OXFORD ENGLISH MEMOIRS AND TRAVELS

General Editor: James Kinsley

Charles Darwin and T. H. Huxley

Autobiographies

CHARLES DARWIN

THOMAS HENRY HUXLEY

Autobiographies

Edited with an Introduction by
Gavin de Beer

LONDON
OXFORD UNIVERSITY PRESS
NEW YORK TORONTO
1974

Oxford University Press, Ely House, London W1.

GLASGOW   NEW YORK   TORONTO   MELBOURNE   WELLINGTON
CAPE TOWN   IBADAN   NAIROBI   DAR ES SALAAM   LUSAKA   ADDIS ABABA
DELHI   BOMBAY   CALCUTTA   MADRAS   KARACHI   LAHORE   DACCA
KUALA LUMPUR   SINGAPORE   HONG KONG   TOKYO

ISBN 0 19 255410 7

Introduction, Notes, Bibliography, Chronologies, and Index
© Oxford University Press 1974

cC

Printed in Great Britain
by W & J Mackay Limited, Chatham

Contents

	Page
Introduction	ix
Acknowledgements	xviii
Note on the Texts	xix
Select Bibliography	xxi
A Chronology of Charles Darwin	xxiii
A Chronology of Thomas Henry Huxley	xxv

CHARLES DARWIN

| Autobiographical Fragment | 3 |
| Autobiography | 8 |

THOMAS HENRY HUXLEY

Notebook: 'Thoughts and Doings'	91
'Autobiography'	100
Speech at the Royal Society Dinner	110

| Explanatory Notes | 113 |
| Index | 120 |

Illustrations

facing page

Erasmus Darwin; Robert Darwin   22

Charles Darwin and his wife, Emma   23

Humboldt; Lyell; Herschel; Henslow   38

H.M.S. *Beagle*   39

Joseph Dalton Hooker; Alfred Russel Wallace   54

Richard Owen   55

Darwin   70

Down House; Darwin's study at Down   71

T. H. Huxley, aged thirty-two   86

H.M.S. *Rattlesnake*   87

Samuel Wilberforce   102

Huxley in later life, and his wife   103

We are grateful to the following for their kind permission to re-produce the illustrations in this book: Mansell Collection: 38 (top left), 55, 70, 71 (top and bottom), 103 (right); National Maritime Museum; 39, 87; Radio Times Hulton Picture Library: 22 (left), 23 (left), 38 (top right), 38 (bottom left), 38 (bottom right), 54 (top and bottom), 86, 102, 103 (left). In the case of the illustrations on pages 22 (right) and 23 (right), we have been unable to trace the copyright holders as these pictures were supplied by the late Sir Gavin de Beer who unfortunately left no record of their source. We hope that any possible owners of these pictures will accept our apologies.

Introduction

'AUTOBIOGRAPHIES are essentially works of fiction, whatever biographies may be', wrote Huxley, by which he did not mean that autobiographies were ephemeral or unreal, but that the auto-biographer, late in life, looking at himself as he thought he had been and was, could see things out of focus with an aberration magnified by hindsight which might lead him astray, or, alternatively, raise commonplace facts on to a higher level of imaginative value.

A common feature of good autobiographies is that they do not lend themselves readily to collation with journals and diaries kept by the writers at earlier times of their lives. An example of this is Edward Gibbon's autobiographical sketches (there were six of them) in one of which he gave a belated birth-certificate of his *Decline and Fall*: 'In my Journal the place and moment of conception are recorded: the fifteenth of October 1764, in the close of the evening as I sat musing in the church of the Zoccolanti or Franciscan Fathers, while they were singing vespers in the Temple of Jupiter.' Alas, his Journal contains no entry at all for 15 October 1764. The passage of time and hindsight had played tricks with Gibbon's memory and history of his own ideas; yet there is no reason to doubt that the event had marked itself more indelibly on his mind than on the pages of his Journal, and that the inaccuracy of his autobiographical sketch was not an untruth.[1]

With Darwin's *Autobiography*, as we shall see, there is a comparable discrepancy between his memory and the day-to-day records of the development of his ideas and thoughts. This is of some importance,

[1] *Gibbon and his World*, by Sir Gavin de Beer, London 1968, p. 62.

for it has led to an inaccurate view of the debt which Darwin owed to Malthus. The transition from Gibbon to Darwin is not far-fetched, for Charles Lyell had the greatest admiration for Gibbon, and Darwin learned much from Lyell. It is Darwin's Notebooks on Transmutation of Species,[2] written between 1837 and 1839, which show that he used more hindsight than he realized in his *Autobiography* when he wrote: 'I happened to read for amusement "Malthus on Population", and being well prepared to appreciate the struggle for existence . . . it at once struck me that under these circumstances favourable variations would tend to be preserved and unfavourable ones to be destroyed' (p. 71 below). From this sentence, unwary commentators have concluded that it was from Malthus that Darwin derived his idea of Natural Selection. Far from it. Darwin already knew, months before he read Malthus, that selection was the key to man's success in breeding and improving cultivated plants and domestic animals, and he was certain that somehow, selection must be responsible in nature for the origin and improvement of adaptation (which constitute evolution) without which plants and animals become extinct. As he wrote to Henry Fawcett,[3] in about 1876, I clearly saw that selection was man's chief means. When I had got 'hus far I strongly suspected that this was the key to nature's work.'

This is completely borne out by Darwin's First Notebook, written between July 1837 and February 1838, where he observed that the southern rhea, not being well adapted, might 'perish out', while another bird (the mocking-bird), being well adapted, would increase and flourish. He went on, 'death of a species is a consequence of non-adaptation'. Here was clear recognition of the importance of favourable variation and efficient adaptation for survival, by natural selection of the more numerous parents of successive generations.

It was on 28 September 1838 that Darwin started to read Malthus.[4]

[2] 'Darwin's Notebooks on Transmutation of Species' [6 parts], edited by Sir Gavin de Beer, *Bulletin of the British Museum* (*Natural History*) Historical Series, vol. 2, 1960, vol. 3, 1967.

[3] Darwin to Henry Fawcett; Sotheby Sale Catalogue, 20 June 1947.

[4] 'Darwin's Notebook on Transmutation of Species III', *Bull. Brit. Mus.* (*Nat. Hist.*) Historical Series, vol. 3, 1967, p. 162.

He at once hit on the passage where it is argued that, the rate of human reproduction being greater than that of increase of human food-supply, the result could only be misery and mortality for the poor.[5] This argument is unsound, because even today nobody knows by how much human food-supplies could be increased if the operation benefited by sufficient priorities and expenditure. But Darwin saw that if applied to mice, birds, or plants, which cannot artificially increase their food-supplies, the result was bound to be heavy mortality, and this explained the inexorable pressure that natural selection brings to bear on those plants and animals which are, even ever so little, better or worse adapted to the environmental conditions in which they live. The former leave more and, by heredity, better-adapted offspring.

Malthus would have been scandalized to learn that his work had played any part at all in the composition of Darwin's demonstration of evolution by natural selection, for it was precisely to combat the subversive views of French revolutionaries who maintained that man was improvable and evolution possible that Malthus wrote his book. All that Darwin derived from Malthus was what has been called an 'analogical leap'[6] from Malthus's fallacious argument on man to a valid argument on plants and animals.[7] This important chapter in the history of ideas has been telescoped in Darwin's *Autobiography*.

There is another field in which old Darwin forgot one of the most important things that had happened to young Darwin: how that academically undistinguished postulant for holy orders, who did not even know what science meant a few weeks before starting on the voyage of the *Beagle*, came back after five years one of the hardest-headed scientists of all time. The general lines of the answer to this

[5] *Essay on the Principle of Population,* by Thomas Robert Malthus, 6th edition, London 1826, vol. 1, p. 6.

[6] 'Evolution and Human Behavior' by Lawrence Zelic Freedman and Anne Roe, *Behavior and Evolution,* edited by Anne Roe and George Gaylord Simpson, New Haven (Conn.) 1958, p. 473.

[7] 'Other Men's Shoulders', by Sir Gavin de Beer, *Annals of Science,* vol. 20, 1965, p. 303.

problem are known,[8] but details remain to be discovered and worked out, in spite of recent books on Darwin and the *Beagle*, where the Darwin quoted is the man of many years later, when he had solved his problem, and not the young man wrestling with observations and meditations which were his formative stimuli.

Darwin started to write his autobiography in 1876, when he was sixty-seven years old, and he added passages to it in 1878 and in 1881. But in 1838 he had written an autobiographical fragment covering the first ten years of his life, on a larger scale than his main *Autobiography*. This fragment, which throws a fuller light on his early years, seems to have been written from memory and notes in August 1838, when he also recapitulated his life up to that time in his Journal.[9] This appears to have been the time when he had decided to propose marriage to his cousin Emma Wedgwood, and he was putting his past in order. The Journal was continued up to two days before he died in 1882; the autobiographical fragment was not continued beyond July 1820. It is reprinted here on pages 3–7.

Huxley's 'Autobiography' was written in 1889 when he was sixty-four years old. It is unfortunately so short that it omits many personal matters, such as his agonized waiting, fighting against the Admiralty, until he could earn a salary on which he could marry and until his betrothed, Henrietta Anne Heathorn, returned to England from Australia where he had met her. There was also the shock when a doctor said that he gave her only six months to live, a prognosis that was wrong by over half a century. And there was the grief of the death of their first-born Noel, not yet four years old, a tragedy that set Huxley's mind working on a criticism of orthodox theology that made him an agnostic—a word which he coined.

Huxley's 'Autobiography' is also silent on details of how he taught himself not only what he knew, but also how to learn. A Notebook which he labelled 'Thoughts and Doings', referring to his life between

[8] 'The Origins of Darwin's Ideas on Evolution and Natural Selection', by Sir Gavin de Beer, *Proceedings of the Royal Society* Series B, vol. 155, 1961, p. 321.

[9] Darwin's Journal, edited by Sir Gavin de Beer, *Bull. Brit. Mus. (Nat. Hist.)* Historical Series, vol. 2, 1959, pages 1-21.

the ages of fifteen and seventeen, gives this information, and it is printed here on pages 91–8. It is astounding how critical his judgment had become at the age of fifteen, how wide his interests, and how great his power of self-discipline, to determine, unaided, the subjects which he decided to learn, and to split them up so as to devise a time-table for their study, while all the time working as assistant to a general practitioner in a desperately poor part of London. A passage from a Journal he kept at that time has been added, for it gives a description of conditions which even his contemporary Charles Dickens could not have surpassed in poignancy, and is very significant for the formation of his opinions.

Although it is concerned with events of Huxley's professional career, his 'Autobiography' omits mention of his epoch-making Croonian Lecture to the Royal Society in 1858, when he utterly demolished the deductive method in anatomical studies and, with it, the reputation of that outrageously dishonest, malicious, and fallacious mandarin Richard Owen.[10] It is also silent on the 'Battle of Oxford',[11] when, in 1860, Huxley came up against the Bishop of Oxford and his prompter Owen and smashed them both, thereby earning the title of 'Darwin's bulldog' and spoiling all attempts of the Church of England to discredit evolution. The shortness of his 'Autobiography' has also made it desirable to reproduce (pages 110–12) his speech at the Anniversary Dinner of the Royal Society on 30 November 1894, the last which he attended before his death. He was then sixty-nine years old, and the clarity and incisiveness of his mind were as trenchant, and as good-natured, as ever.

Comparison between the two autobiographies is revealing of the characters of their authors, and each to some extent bears on and helps to interpret the other, which is the reason for their inclusion together in this volume. Darwin had no lack of fun, as is seen in his

[10] *Charles Darwin*, by Sir Gavin de Beer, London 1963, pp. 165, 262, gives examples of Owen's behaviour.

[11] Huxley's own description of the 'Battle of Oxford' is in his letter to F. D. Dyster of 9 September 1860, printed in 'Charles Darwin. Lecture on a Master Mind', by Sir Gavin de Beer, *Proceedings of the British Academy*, vol. 44, 1958, p. 18.

letters. For instance, he accepted John Jenner Weir's invitation to become a Patron of the Cat Show, but warned him that 'people may refuse to go and admire a lot of atheistical cats'.[12] But his account of himself shows a certain ponderousness of opinion and of judgment, and a dumb sagacity which moved surely but slowly.

Huxley's writing about himself is replete with wry wit, lightning rapidity of thought, and a readiness to take the gloves off. Allowance must, of course, be made for the difference between the conditions under which Darwin's and Huxley's texts came to be written. Darwin's was a family document, written it is true at the suggestion of a German publisher (who, whoever he was, does not seem to have published it), but principally to amuse himself and to interest his children and their children. Huxley's 'Autobiography' was written specifically in response to an invitation, long refused, to write an account of his life, acceded to only because he realized that if he did not write it himself, the importunate editor would write and publish something that might be 'all wrong'.

Darwin was well aware of the razor-blade sharpness of his great friend's power of analysis and the speed of his thought. In 1862 Huxley had given six weekly lectures, extempore, on subjects connected with the origin of species, and they were published in pamphlet form, week by week, by one of his fascinated listeners.[13] Darwin read them and wrote to Huxley,[14] in his spirit of friendly banter, but ruefully conscious of the hard labour that the *Origin of Species* had cost him, 'They are simply perfect. They ought to be largely advertised; but it is very good of me to say so, for I threw down No. IV with this reflection, "What is the good of writing a

[12] Darwin to John Jenner Weir, 18 September 1872; Sotheby Sale Catalogue, 24 July 1916.

[13] *On our Knowledge of the Causes of the Phenomena of Organic Nature,* by Thomas Henry Huxley, published in six weekly parts, with permission, by J. Aldous Mays, London 1862; reprinted as *On the Origin of Species or, The Causes of the Phenomena of Organic Nature,* by Thomas Henry Huxley, Introduction by Ashley Montagu, Ann Arbor (Mich.) 1968.

[14] Darwin to Huxley, 18 December 1862, *Life and Letters of Thomas Henry Huxley,* by Leonard Huxley, London 1900, vol. 1, p. 207.

thundering big book, when everything is in this green little book, so despicable for its size?" In the name of all that is good and bad, I may as well shut up shop altogether.'

Within two months of his death Darwin wrote to John Collier,[15] referring to Huxley's *Essays*:

That on automatism is wonderfully interesting, more is the pity say I, for if I were as well armed as Huxley I would challenge him to a duel on this subject. But I am a deal too wise to do anything of the kind, for he would run me through the body half a dozen times with his sharp and polished rapier before I knew where I was.

Huxley's opinion of Darwin was one of immense admiration and respect, though he never abandoned his almost puritanical critical judgment and entered caveats here and there. His famous remark when he read the *Origin of Species*, 'How extremely stupid not to have thought of that', conceded victory to the slower-minded man, and his letter to Darwin of 23 November 1859[16] was a far-sighted declaration of allegiance and alliance:

I trust you will not allow yourself to be in any way disgusted or annoyed by the considerable abuse and misrepresentation which, unless I greatly mistake, is in store for you. Depend on it you have earned the lasting gratitude of all thoughtful men. As to the curs which will bark and yelp, you must recollect that some of your friends, at any rate, are endowed with a combativeness which (though you have often and justly rebuked it) may stand you in good stead. I am sharpening up my claws and beak in readiness.

Darwin and Huxley resembled each other because not only had they been 'well salted in early life' by their experiences on dangerous voyages under the White Ensign, but they had no systematic instruction in biology at all, and they learnt it the hard way. Where they differed was in their own development of thought and interests. As

[15] Darwin to John Collier, 16 February 1882, Sotheby Sale Catalogue, 14 November 1934, Lot 611.

[16] *Life and Letters of Thomas Henry Huxley*, by Leonard Huxley, London 1900, vol. 1, p. 176.

soon as he saw his way to prove the fact of evolution by natural
selection, Darwin had little room in his mind for anything else, and
he knew it. As he wrote[17] to J. D. Hooker when he was struggling
with the *Origin of Species*, 'It is an accursed evil to a man to become so
absorbed in any subject as I am in mine.' His beam of concentrated
attention was, for the rest of his life, focused on what he could find
that bore on evolution and natural selection. So completely was he
enthralled by his subject that he practically invented his own method
of getting information, first by circulating printed questionnaires,
and next, when he found anybody who possessed the knowledge
that he wanted, by writing letter after letter with question after
question, disarmingly interspersed with 'If it would not cause you
too much trouble', 'Pray add to your kindness', 'I fear that you will
think that you have fallen on a most troublesome petitioner'. His
correspondents must have felt their hearts sink when the postman
brought them a letter with the Downe postmark.[18] He knew very
well what a nuisance he was being, and admitted it to Jenner Weir:[19]
'If any man wants to gain a good opinion of his fellow men, he
ought to do what I am doing, pester them with letters.' Nothing
must be allowed to stand in the way of the One Great Subject, and
this is why his achievement was so great.

Huxley's mental development was quite different. From an early
and deeply ingrained interest in engineering, he moved to medicine
and that biological engineering which is physiology. His interest in
biology, comparative anatomy and palaeontology, he never lost, but
in his forties his interests took him into wider spheres, especially
education and ethics, both of which reflected the effect produced on
his mind by Darwin and the *Origin of Species*. The first of these

[17] Darwin to J. D. Hooker, 13 October 1858, *Life and Letters of Charles Darwin*,
edited by Francis Darwin, London 1887, vol. 2, p. 139.

[18] Examples of Darwin's method are given in *Questions about the Breeding of
Animals*, by Charles Darwin, Introduction by Sir Gavin de Beer, Society for the
Bibliography of Natural History, Sherborn Fund Facsimile Number 3, London
1968.

[19] Darwin to J. Jenner Weir, 6 March 1868, Sotheby Sale Catalogue, 29 March
1922.

interests was recognized officially by his appointment to the London School Board, where he was responsible for a greater influence on the policy of national elementary education than had any other man. There he astonished the enemies that he had made through his uncompromising defence of evolution and natural selection and his denial of divine design in nature, by advocating continuance of the teaching of the Bible, partly because of its literary value, but mostly because he was 'seriously perplexed to know by what practical measure the religious feeling, which is the essential basis of conduct, was to be kept up in the present utterly chaotic state of opinion in these matters, without its use'.[20] This was in 1870.

It should not surprise any reader that Huxley set so much store by religion: he was a deeply religious man but he could not bear theology with its dogmatism, its alleged revelations, and its clutter of scientifically disproved or unprovable assertions. Always pursuing his puritanical principle of respecting the order of nature and 'the universal validity of the law of causation',[21] he made his own position plain when he wrote[22] 'there is no evidence of the existence of such a being as the God of theologians', while he asserted that 'atheism is on purely philosophical grounds untenable'. In place of both views he advanced the principle of agnosticism,[23] by which he meant the subordination of belief to evidence and reason. His fight against the opposition to the gospel that flowed from the *Origin of Species*, always mellowed by sweet reasonableness, was the spearhead of the 'movement of opinion which has been called the New Reformation', words which end his 'Autobiography', though the movement goes on and gains speed.

[20] T. H. Huxley, *Collected Essays*, 3, 'Science and Education', London 1893, p. 397.

[21] T. H. Huxley, *Collected Essays*, 9, 'Evolution and Ethics', London 1894, p. 121.

[22] *Life and Letters of Thomas Henry Huxley,* by Leonard Huxley, London 1900, vol. 2, p. 162.

[23] First formulated in Huxley's letter to Charles Kingsley, 23 September 1860; *Life and Letters of Thomas Henry Huxley* by Leonard Huxley, London 1900, vol. 1, pp. 217-22.

Darwin also acknowledged himself an agnostic and made the splendid remark: 'Considering how fiercely I have been attacked by the orthodox, it seems ludicrous that I once intended to be a clergyman' (p. 31 below). His achievement did not prevent his burial in Westminster Abbey, and it is impossible to resist asking the question why Huxley, after his enormous services to science and the State, recognized by his appointment as Privy Councillor, was not also buried there.

Lastly, what is the position of the autobiographies in the works of Darwin and Huxley? They add little to science, but they do add enormously to our understanding of the lives, qualities, and humanity of two incomparable scientists.

Acknowledgements

FOR the inclusion in this volume of the texts of Darwin's Autobiographical Fragment and his *Autobiography* grateful acknowledgement is made to Mr. George Darwin and the Librarian of the Cambridge University Library; similarly for Huxley's 'Autobiography', 'Thoughts and Doings', and Speech, thanks are due to Mrs. Rosalind Huxley, Sir Julian Huxley, and to the Rector and the Archivist of the Imperial College of Science and Technology.

For information on various points, the Editor expresses his thanks to Sir Julian Huxley, Sir Basil Blackwell, Mrs. Jeanne Pingree, College Archivist of the Imperial College of Science and Technology, Mr. Ronald W. Clark, Professor James Kinsley, and Mr. M. J. Rowlands, Librarian of the British Museum (Natural History).

Note on the Texts

DARWIN'S short autobiographical sketch, written in 1838 and covering only the early years of his life, was published in *More Letters of Charles Darwin* (John Murray) in 1903. Most of his *Autobiography* was written between 31 May and 3 August 1876, but he made additions to the text in 1878 and 1881. It was first published in *Life and Letters of Charles Darwin*, ed. Francis Darwin (John Murray, 1887), and a passage about his mother in *More Letters of Charles Darwin*, ed. Francis Darwin and A. C. Seward (John Murray, 1903). The text of that published *Autobiography* was designedly incomplete, because Darwin's widow and some of his children objected to the publication of passages in which Darwin criticized orthodox theology and expressed his inability to accept it.

In the 1887 edition, the passage relating to Darwin's father was given in a different chapter from the remainder of the *Autobiography*, and when this was reprinted in The Thinker's Library (Watts & Co., 1929) this passage was omitted and the remainder of the *Autobiography* was still incomplete, as it was also in the edition by George Gaylord Simpson (New York: Henry Schuman) in 1950.

It was not until 1958 that a complete, critical, unexpurgated edition (Collins) was prepared by Nora Barlow, Darwin's granddaughter, revised from the original (and difficult) manuscript in Cambridge University Library (Darwin Papers 26). The present text has been established by James Kinsley from a fresh collation of this manuscript, with some silent editorial emendations.

HUXLEY'S 'Autobiography', written in 1889, was published by

Louis Engel in a book with the unlikely title of *From Handel to Hallé: Biographical Sketches with Autobiographies of Professor Huxley and Professor Herkomer,* 1890; the manuscript is not traced. It was also printed in *Collected Essays,* i, 1893. Extracts from the 'Autobiography' were included in Leonard Huxley's *Life and Letters of Thomas Henry Huxley* (Macmillan, 1900). Huxley's Notebook 'Thoughts and Doings', from which passages were also used by Leonard Huxley, has been transcribed from the manuscript (Huxley Papers, 31. 169) in the Archives of the Imperial College of Science and Technology. The short extract from a journal which is printed here, following 'Thoughts and Doings', is from Leonard Huxley's book (i. 15, 16) where its provenance is not given. Huxley's speech at the Anniversary Dinner of the Royal Society was printed in the same work, taken from *The Times* of 1 December 1894.

Select Bibliography
(Biographical)

CHARLES DARWIN

Life and Letters of Charles Darwin, ed. Francis Darwin, 3 vols. (1887).

More Letters of Charles Darwin, ed. Francis Darwin and A. C. Seward, 2 vols. (1903).

H. E. Litchfield, *Emma Darwin*, 2 vols. (1904).

The Autobiography of Charles Darwin, ed. Nora Barlow (1958).

Charles Darwin's Diary of the Voyage of the Beagle, ed. Nora Barlow (1934).

Charles Darwin and the Voyage of the Beagle, ed. Nora Barlow (1945).

Sketch of 1842 and Essay of 1844 in Charles Darwin and Alfred Russel Wallace: *Evolution by Natural Selection*, ed. Sir Gavin de Beer, Cambridge (1958).

Sir Gavin de Beer, *Charles Darwin. Evolution by Natural Selection* (1963).

'Darwin's Journal', ed. Sir Gavin de Beer, *Bulletin of the British Museum (Natural History)*, Historical Series, ii (1959), 1-21.

'Darwin's Notebooks on Transmutation of Species', Parts I-IV, ed. Sir Gavin de Beer (Parts V & VI with M. J. Rowlands, Part VI with B. M. Skramovsky); *Bulletin of the British Museum (Natural History)*, Historical Series, ii (1960), 23-200; iii (1967), 129-76.

Sir Gavin de Beer, 'Mendel, Darwin, and Fisher', *Notes and Records of the Royal Society*, xix (1964), 192-226; xxi (1966), 64-71.

Saul Adler, 'Darwin's Illness', *Nature*, London, clxxxiv (1959), 1102-3.

Note: Darwin's more important publications, including his books, are referred to in the *Autobiography* and are included in his Chronology under the relevant dates (pp. xxiii–xxiv below).

THOMAS HENRY HUXLEY

Louis Engel, *From Handel to Hallé* (1890), pp. 121-34.

Leonard Huxley, *Life and Letters of Thomas Henry Huxley*, 2 vols. (1900).

Thomas Henry Huxley's Diary of the Voyage of H.M.S. Rattlesnake, ed. Julian Huxley (1935).

Collected Essays of Thomas Henry Huxley, 9 vols. (1893-4).

The Scientific Memoirs of Thomas Henry Huxley, ed. M. Foster and E. Ray Lankester, 5 vols. (1898-1903).

Ronald W. Clark, *The Huxleys* (1968).

Note: Huxley's more important publications, including his books, are included in his Chronology under the relevant dates (pp. xxv–xxvi below).

A Chronology of Charles Darwin

		Age
1809	(12 February) Born at Shrewsbury, son of Robert Waring Darwin and Suzannah *née* Wedgwood	
1817	Attended Dr. G. Case's day school at Shrewsbury	8
1818	Entered Shrewsbury School	9
1825	(22 October) Matriculated in University of Edinburgh	16
1827	(15 October) Admitted to Christ's College, Cambridge	18
1831	Graduated B.A. (August) Received invitation to sail in the *Beagle*. (27 December) H.M.S. *Beagle* sailed from Plymouth	22
1835	Visited Galapagos Islands	26
1836	(2 October) Landed at Falmouth	27
1837	(July) Opened First Notebook on Transmutation of Species	28
1838	(28 September) Read Malthus on *Population*	29
1839	(1 January) Established at 12 Upper Gower Street. (24 January) Elected F.R.S. (29 January) Married Emma Wedgwood at Maer, Staffs.; (August) *Journal of Researches into the Geology and Natural History* (of the voyage of the *Beagle*) published; (27 December) William Erasmus Darwin born	30
1842	(May) Wrote Sketch of Species Theory; *Structure and Distribution of Coral Reefs* published. (17 September) Moved to Down House, Downe, Kent	33
1844	(July) Wrote Essay on Species Theory; *Geological Observations on Volcanic Islands* published	35
1845	*Journal of Researches into the Natural History and Geology* [*sic*] (of the voyage of the *Beagle*) published	36
1846	*Geological Observations on South America* published	37
1851	*Monograph of Fossil Lepadidae published* (barnacles); *Monograph of* [recent] *Lepadidae* published	42

1853 Awarded Royal Medal of the Royal Society   44

1854 *Monograph of* [recent] *Balanidae* published; *Monograph of Fossil Balanidae* published   45

1856 Began to write large work on Species   47

1858 (18 June) Received from Alfred Russel Wallace a perfect summary of his own theory of evolution by natural selection. (1 July) Joint paper with Wallace read before Linnean Society of London   49

1859 (24 November) *On the Origin of Species* published   50

1860 (7 January) *Origin* (2nd edition) published   51

1861 (April) *Origin* (3rd edition) published   52

1862 *On the various contrivances by which British and Foreign Orchids are Fertilised by Insects* published   53

1864 Awarded Copley Medal of the Royal Society   55

1866 (15 December) *Origin* (4th edition) published   57

1868 *Variation of Animal and Plants under Domestication* published   59

1869 (7 August) *Origin* (5th edition) published   60

1871 (24 February) *Descent of Man* published   62

1872 (19 February) *Origin* (6th edition) published; (26 November) *The Expression of the Emotions in Man and Animals* published   63

1875 (2 July) *Insectivorous Plants* published; (September) *Climbing Plants* published   66

1876 *Effects of Cross- and Self-Fertilisation in the Vegetable Kingdom* published   67

1877 *Different forms of flowers on plants of the same Species* published   68

1879 *Life of Erasmus Darwin* published   70

1880 *Power of Movement in Plants* published   71

1881 *Formation of Vegetable Mould through the action of Worms* published   72

1882 (19 April) Died at Down House. (26 April) Buried in Westminster Abbey   73

A Chronology of Thomas Henry Huxley

Age

1825 (4 May) Born at Ealing, son of George Huxley and Rachel *née* Withers

1833 Attended Ealing School under his schoolmaster father   8

1835 Left school (which closed); went to Coventry   10

1839 Introduced to medicine by Dr. Cooke   14

1841 Became assistant to Dr. Chandler at Rotherhithe   16

1842 Moved to North London as apprentice to Dr. George Salt and entered Charing Cross Hospital Medical School   17

1845 M.B., London University; 'On a hitherto undescribed Structure in the Human Hair-Sheath' (*Medical Gazette*) published   20

1846 Posted to Haslar Hospital as Lieutenant, R.N. Medical Service; (3 December) sailed from Portsmouth in H.M.S. *Rattlesnake* as Assistant Surgeon, to survey Australasian waters   21

1847 Met Henrietta Anne Heathorn at Sydney   22

1849 'On the Anatomy and Affinities of the Medusae' (*Philosophical Transactions of the Royal Society*) published   24

1850 (23 October) H.M.S. *Rattlesnake* reached Plymouth   25

1851 (5 June) Elected F.R.S.   26

1852 (30 November) Awarded Royal Medal of the Royal Society   27

1854 Appointed Lecturer in Natural History at Government School of Mines; Lecturer in Comparative Anatomy at St. Thomas's Hospital; Lecturer in the Department of Science and Art, South Kensington; *On the Educational value of the Natural History Sciences* published   29

1855 (March) Appointed Naturalist to the Geological Survey;

(21 July) Married Henrietta Anne Heathorn, at All Saints, Maida Vale, established at 14 Waverley Place   30

1856 Visited Switzerland with John Tyndall to study the structure of glaciers   31

1858 Delivered the Croonian Lecture 'On the Theory of the Vertebrate Skull', *Proceedings of the Royal Society,* ix (1858), 381   33

1859 *The Oceanic Hydrozoa* published. (26 December) Review of the *Origin of Species* published in *The Times*   34

1860 (30 June) Meeting of the British Association for the Advancement of Science, Oxford, victory for Darwin. Moved to 26 Abbey Place; (11 December) Leonard Huxley born   35

1863 *Evidence as to Man's place in Nature* published   38

1864 *Lectures on the Elements of Comparative Anatomy* published   39

1866 *Lessons in Elementary Physiology* published   41

1870 Appointed to London School Board   45

1871 Appointed Secretary of the Royal Society   46

1872 Moved to Marlborough Place. Breakdown in health   47

1873 Received £2,100 from friends to enable him to take a complete rest; visited Auvergne   48

1876 Visited U.S.A.   51

1877 *Manual of the Anatomy of Invertebrated Animals* published   52

1878 Hon. LL.D., Dublin   53

1880 *The Crayfish* published   55

1882 *Manual of the Anatomy of Vertebrated Animals* published   57

1883 Elected President of the Royal Society   58

1885 Hon. D.C.L., Oxford   60

1890 Moved to 'Hodeslea', Eastbourne   65

1892 Appointed Privy Councillor   67

1893 Delivered the Romanes Lecture on *Evolution and Ethics* at Oxford   68

1895 (29 June) Died at Eastbourne. (3 July) Buried at Finchley   70

CHARLES DARWIN

An Autobiographical Fragment, Written in 1838

===

MY earliest recollection, the date of which I can approximately tell, and which must have been before I was four years old, was when sitting on Caroline's[1] knee in the drawing room, whilst she was cutting an orange for me, a cow ran by the window which made me jump, so that I received a bad cut, of which I bear the scar to this day. Of this scene I recollect the place where I sat and the cause of the fright, but not the cut itself, and I think my memory is real, and not as often happens in similar cases, [derived] from hearing the thing often repeated, [when] one obtains so vivid an image, that it cannot be separated from memory: because I clearly remember which way the cow ran, which would not probably have been told me. My memory here is an obscure picture, in which from not recollecting any pain I am scarcely conscious of its reference to myself.

1813. When I was four years and a half old I went to the sea, and stayed there some weeks. I remember many things, but with the exception of the maidservants (and these are not individualised) I recollect none of my family who were there. I remember either myself or Catherine[2] being naughty, and being shut up in a room and trying to break the windows. I have an obscure picture of a house before my eyes, and of a neighbouring small shop, where the owner gave me one fig, but which to my great joy turned out to be two: this fig was given me that the man might kiss the maidservant. I remember a common walk to a kind of well, on the road to which was a cottage shaded with damascene trees, inhabited by an old man, called a hermit, with white hair, who used to give us damascenes.[3] I know not whether the damascenes, or the reverence and indistinct fear for this old man produced the greatest effect on my memory.

3

I remember when going there crossing in the carriage a broad ford, and fear and astonishment of white foaming water has made a vivid impression. I think memory of events commences abruptly; that is, I remember these earliest things quite as clearly as others very much later in life, which were equally impressed on me. Some very early recollections are connected with fear at Parkfield[1] and with poor Betty Harvey. I remember with horror her story of people being pushed into the canal by the towing rope, by going the wrong side of the horse. I had the greatest horror of this story—keen instinct against death. Some other recollections are those of vanity—namely, thinking that people were admiring me, in one instance for perseverance and another for boldness in climbing a low tree, and what is odder, a consciousness, as if instinctive, that I was vain, and contempt of myself. My supposed admirer was old Peter Haile the bricklayer, and the tree the mountain ash on the lawn. All my recollections seem to be connected most closely with myself; now Catherine seems to recollect scenes where others were the chief actors. When my mother[2] died I was 8½ years old, and [Catherine] one year less, yet she remembers all particulars and events of each day whilst I scarcely recollect anything (and so with very many other cases) except being sent for, the memory of going into her room, my father meeting me —crying afterwards. I recollect my mother's gown and scarcely anything of her appearance, except one or two walks with her. I have no distinct remembrance of any conversation, and those only of a very trivial nature. I remember her saying 'if she did ask me to do something,' which I said she had, 'it was solely for my good.'

Catherine remembers my mother crying, when she heard of my grandmother's death. Also when at Parkfield how Aunt Sarah[3] and Aunt Kitty used to receive her. Susan,[4] like me, only remembers affairs personal. It is sufficiently odd this [difference] in subjects remembered. Catherine says she does not remember the impression made upon her by external things, as scenery, but for things which she reads she has an excellent memory, *i.e.,* for ideas. Now her sympathy being ideal, it is part of her character, and shows how easily

4

her kind of memory was stamped, a vivid thought is repeated, a vivid impression forgotten.

I remember obscurely the illumination after the battle of Waterloo, and the Militia exercising about that period, in the field opposite our house.

1817. At $8\frac{1}{2}$ years old I went to Mr. Case's School.[1] I remember how very much I was afraid of meeting the dogs in Barker Street, and how at school I could not get up my courage to fight. I was very timid by nature. I remember I took great delight at school in fishing for newts in the quarry pool. I had thus young formed a strong taste for collecting, chiefly seals, franks, etc., but also pebbles and minerals—one which was given me by some boy decided this taste. I believe shortly after this, or before, I had smattered in botany, and certainly when at Mr. Case's School I was very fond of gardening, and invented some great falsehoods about being able to colour crocuses[2] as I liked. At this time I felt very strong friendship for some boys. It was soon after I began collecting stones, *i.e.,* when 9 or 10, that I distinctly recollect the desire I had of being able to know something about every pebble in front of the hall door—it was my earliest and only geological aspiration at that time. I was in those days a very great story-teller— for the pure pleasure of exciting attention and surprise. I stole fruit and hid it for these same motives, and injured trees by barking them for similar ends. I scarcely ever went out walking without saying I had seen a pheasant or some strange bird (natural history taste); these lies, when not detected, I presume, excited my attention, as I recollect them vividly, not connected with shame, though some I do, but as something which by having produced a great effect on my mind, gave pleasure like a tragedy. I recollect when I was at Mr. Case's inventing a whole fabric to show how fond I was of speaking the *truth*! My invention is still so vivid in my mind, that I could almost fancy it was true, did not memory of former shame tell me it was false. I have no particularly happy or unhappy recollections of this time or earlier periods of my life. I remember well a walk I took with a boy named Ford across some fields to a farmhouse on the Church Stretton road. I do not remember any mental pursuits excepting those of collecting stones, etc., gardening, and about this time often going with my father in his carriage, telling him of my lessons, and seeing game and other wild birds, which was a great delight to me. I was born a naturalist.

When I was 9½ years old (July 1818) I went with Erasmus[1] to see Liverpool: it has left no impressions on my mind, except most trifling ones—fear of the coach upsetting, a good dinner, and an extremely vague memory of ships.

In Midsummer of this year I went to Dr. Butler's School.[2] I well recollect the first going there, which oddly enough I cannot of going to Mr. Case's, the first school of all. I remember the year 1818 well, not from having first gone to a public school, but from writing those figures in my school book, accompanied with obscure thoughts, now fulfilled, whether I should recollect in future life that year.

In September (1818) I was ill with the scarlet fever. I well remember the wretched feeling of being delirious.

1819, July (10½ years old). Went to the sea at Plas Edwards[3] and stayed there three weeks, which now appears to me like three months. I remember a certain shady green road (where I saw a snake) and a waterfall, with a degree of pleasure, which must be connected with the pleasure from scenery, though not directly recognised as such. The sandy plain before the house has left a strong impression, which is obscurely connected with an indistinct remembrance of curious insects, probably a *Cimex* mottled with red, and *Zygæna*, the burnet-moth. I was at that time very passionate (when I swore like a trooper) and quarrelsome. The former passion has I think nearly wholly but slowly died away. When journeying there by stage coach I remember a recruiting officer (I think I should know his face to this day) at tea time, asking the maid-servant for toasted bread and butter. I was convulsed with laughter and thought it the quaintest and wittiest speech that ever passed from the mouth of man. Such is wit at 10½ years old. The memory now flashes across me of the pleasure I had in the evening on a blowy day walking along the beach by myself and seeing the gulls and cormorants wending their way home in a wild and irregular course. Such poetic pleasures, felt so keenly in after years, I should not have expected so early in life.

1820, July. Went a riding tour (on old Dobbin) with Erasmus to Pistyll Rhiadr[1]; of this I recollect little, an indistinct picture of the fall, but I well remember my astonishment on hearing that fishes could jump up it.

Autobiography

===

May 31st, 1876
Recollections of the Development of my mind and character

A GERMAN editor having written to me to ask for an account of the development of my mind and character with some sketch of my autobiography, I have thought that the attempt would amuse me, and might possibly interest my children or their children. I know that it would have interested me greatly to have read even so short and dull a sketch of the mind of my grandfather written by himself, and what he thought and did and how he worked. I have attempted to write the following account of myself, as if I were a dead man in another world looking back at my own life. Nor have I found this difficult, for life is nearly over with me. I have taken no pains about my style of writing.

I was born at Shrewsbury on February 12th 1809. I have heard my Father[1] say that he believed that persons with powerful minds generally had memories extending back to a very early period of life. This is not my case, for my earliest recollection goes back only to when I was a few months over four years old, when we went to near Abergele for sea-bathing, and I recollect some events and places there with some little distinctness.

My mother[2] died in July 1817, when I was a little over eight years old, and it is odd that I can remember hardly anything about her, except her death-bed, her black velvet gown and her curiously con-structed work-table. I believe that my forgetfulness is partly due to my sisters owing to their great grief never being able to speak about her or mention her name; and partly to her previous invalid state. In the spring of this same year I was sent to a day-school in Shrews-bury,[3] where I staid a year. Before going to school I was educated by my sister Caroline but I doubt whether this plan answered. I have been told that I was much slower in learning than my younger sister

Catherine, and I believe that I was in many ways a naughty boy. Caroline was extremely kind, clever and zealous; but she was too zealous in trying to improve me; for I clearly remember after this long interval of years, saying to myself when about to enter a room where she was—'What will she blame me for now?' and I made myself dogged so as not to care what she might say.

By the time I went to this day-school my taste for natural history, and more especially for collecting, was well developed. I tried to make out the names of plants, and collected all sorts of things, shells, seals, franks, coins and minerals. The passion for collecting, which leads a man to be a systematic naturalist, a virtuoso or a miser, was very strong in me, and was clearly innate, as none of my sisters or brother ever had this taste.

One little event during this year has fixed itself very firmly in my mind, and I hope that it has done so from my conscience having been afterwards sorely troubled by it. it is curious as showing that apparently I was interested at this early age in the variability of plants! I told another little boy (I believe it was Leighton, who afterwards became a well-known Lichenologist and botanist) that I could produce variously coloured Polyanthuses and Primroses by watering them with certain coloured fluids, which was of course a monstrous fable, and had never been tried by me. I may here also confess that as a little boy I was much given to inventing deliberate falsehoods and this was always done for the sake of causing excitement. For instance I once gathered much valuable fruit from my Father's trees and hid them in the shrubbery, and then ran in breathless haste to spread the news that I had discovered a hoard of stolen fruit.

About this time, or as I hope at a somewhat earlier age, I sometimes stole fruit for the sake of eating it; and one of my schemes was ingenious. The kitchen garden was generally kept locked in the evening and was surrounded by a high wall, but by the aid of neighbouring trees I could easily get on the coping. I then fixed a long stick into the hole at the bottom of a rather large flower-pot, and by dragging this upwards pulled off peaches and plums, which fell into the pot and the prizes were thus secured. When a very little boy I remember stealing apples from the orchard, for the sake of giving away to some boys and young men, who lived in a cottage not far off, but before I gave them the fruit I showed off how quickly I could run and it is wonderful that I did not perceive that the surprise and admiration which they expressed at my powers of running, was given for the sake of the apples. But I well remember that I was delighted at them declaring that they had never seen a boy run so fast!

I remember clearly only one other incident during the years whilst at Mr. Case's daily school—namely, the burial of a dragoon-soldier; and it is surprising how clearly I can still see the horse with the man's empty boots and carbine suspended to the saddle, and the firing over the grave. This scene deeply stirred whatever poetic fancy there was in me.

In the summer of 1818 I went to Dr. Butler's[1] great school in Shrewsbury, and remained there for 7 years till midsummer of 1825, when I was 16 years old. I boarded at this school, so that I had the great advantage of living the life of a true school-boy, but as the distance was hardly more than a mile to my home, I very often ran there in the longer intervals between the callings over and before locking up at night. This I think was in many ways advantageous to me by keeping up home affections and interests. I remember in the early part of my school life that I often had to run very quickly to be in time, and from being a fleet runner was generally successful; but when in doubt I prayed earnestly to God to help me, and I well remember that I attributed my success to the prayers and not to my quick running, and marvelled how generally I was aided.

I have heard my Father and elder sisters say that I had as a very young boy a strong taste for long solitary walks; but what I thought about I know not. I often became quite absorbed, and once whilst returning to school on the summit of the old fortifications round Shrewsbury, which had been converted into a public foot-path with no parapet on one side, I walked off and fell to the ground, but the height was only 7 or 8 feet. Nevertheless the number of thoughts which passed through my mind during this very short, but sudden and wholly unexpected fall, was astonishing, and seem hardly compatible with what physiologists have, I believe, proved about each thought requiring quite an appreciable amount of time.

I must have been a very simple little fellow when I first went to the school. A boy of the name of Garnett took me into a cake-shop one day, and bought some cakes for which he did not pay, as the shopman trusted him. When we came out, I asked him why he did not pay for them, and he instantly answered, 'Why, do you not know that my uncle left a great sum of money to the Town on condition that every tradesman should give whatever was wanted without payment to anyone who wore his old hat and moved it in a particular manner;' and he then showed me how it was moved. He then went into another shop where he was trusted, and asked for some small article, moving his hat in the proper manner, and of course obtained it without payment. When we came out he said, 'Now if you like to go by yourself into that cake-shop (how well I remember its exact position) I will lend you my hat and you can get whatever you like if you move the hat on your head properly.' I gladly accepted the generous offer, and went in and asked for some cakes, moved the old hat and was walking out of the shop, when the shop-man made a rush at me, so I dropped the cakes and ran away for dear life, and was astonished by being greeted with shouts of laughter by my false friend Garnett.

I can say in my own favour that I was as a boy humane, but I owed this entirely to the instruction and example of my sisters. I doubt indeed whether humanity is a natural or innate quality. I was very fond of collecting eggs, but I never took more than a single egg out of a bird's nest, except on one single occasion, when I took all, not for their value, but from a sort of bravado.

I had a strong taste for angling and would sit for any number of hours on the bank of a river or pond watching the float; when at Maer[1] I was told that I could kill the worms with salt and water, and from that day I never spitted a living worm, though at the expense, probably, of some loss of success.

Once as a very little boy, whilst at the day-school or before that time, I acted cruelly, for I beat a puppy I believe, simply from enjoying the sense of power; but the beating could not have been severe, for the puppy did not howl, of which I feel sure as the spot was near to the house. This act lay heavily on my conscience, as is shown by my remembering the exact spot where the crime was committed. It probably lay all the heavier from my love of dogs being then and for a long time afterwards a passion. Dogs seemed to know this, for I was an adept in robbing their love from their masters.

Nothing could have been worse for the development of my mind than Dr. Butler's school, as it was strictly classical, nothing else being taught except a little ancient geography and history. The school as a means of education to me was simply a blank. During my whole life I have been singularly incapable of mastering any language. Especial attention was paid to verse-making, and this I could never do well. I had many friends and got together a grand collection of old verses, which by patching together, sometimes aided by other boys, I could work into any subject. Much attention was paid to learning by heart the lessons of the previous day; this I could effect with great facility learning 40 or 50 lines of Virgil or Homer, whilst I was in morning chapel; but this exercise was utterly useless for every verse was forgotten in 48 hours. I was not idle, and with the exception of versification generally worked conscientiously at my classics, not using cribs. The sole pleasure I ever received from such studies, was from some of the odes of Horace, which I admired greatly. When I left the school I was for my age neither high nor low in it; and I believe that I was considered by all my masters and by my Father as a very ordinary boy, rather below the common standard in intellect. To my deep mortification my Father once said to me, 'You care for nothing but shooting, dogs and rat-catching, and you will be a disgrace to yourself and all your family.' But my father, who was the kindest man I ever knew, and whose memory I love with all my heart, must have been angry and somewhat unjust when he used such words.

I may here add a few pages about my Father, who was in many

ways a remarkable man. He was about 6 feet 2 inches in height, with broad shoulders and very corpulent, so that he was the largest man, whom I ever saw. When he last weighed himself, he was 24 stone, but afterwards increased much in weight. His chief mental characteristics were his powers of observation and his sympathy, neither of which have I ever seen exceeded or even equalled. His sympathy was not only with the distresses of others, but in a greater degree with the pleasures of all around him. This led him to be always scheming to give pleasure to others, and though hating extravagance to perform many generous actions. For instance, Mr. B. a small manufacturer in Shrewsbury came to him one day, and said he should be bankrupt unless he could at once borrow £10,000, but that he was unable to give any legal security. My Father heard his reasons for believing that he could ultimately repay the money, and from my father's intuitive perception of character felt sure that he was to be trusted. So he advanced this sum, which was a very large one for him while young, and was after a time repaid.

I suppose that it was his sympathy which gave him unbounded power of winning confidence, and as a consequence made him highly successful as a physician. He began to practice before he was 21 years old, and his fees during the first year paid for the keep of two horses and a servant. On the following year his practice was larger and so continued for above 60 years, when he ceased to attend on any one. His great success as a doctor was the more remarkable as he told me that he at first hated his profession so much that if he had been sure of the smallest pittance, or if his Father had given him any choice, nothing should have induced him to follow it. To the end of his life, the thought of an operation almost sickened him, and he could scarcely endure to see a person bled, — a horror which he has transmitted to me, and I remember the horror which I felt as a schoolboy in reading about Pliny (I think) bleeding to death in a warm bath. My Father told me two odd stories about bleeding: one was that as a very young man he became a Free-mason. A friend of his who was a free-mason and who pretended not to know about his strong feeling with respect to blood, remarked casually to him, as they walked to the meeting, 'I suppose that you do not care about losing a few drops of blood?' It seems that when he was received as a member, his eyes were bandaged and his coat-sleeves turned up. Whether any such ceremony is now performed I know not, but my Father mentioned the case as an excellent instance of the power of imagination, for he distinctly felt the blood trickling down his arm, and could hardly believe his own eyes, when he afterwards could not find the smallest prick on his arm.

A great slaughtering butcher from London once consulted my grandfather, when another man very ill was brought in, and my grandfather wished to have him instantly bled by the accompanying apothecary. The butcher was asked to hold the patient's arm, but he made some excuse and left the room. Afterwards he explained to my grandfather that although he believed that he had killed with his own hands more animals than any other man in London, yet absurd as it might seem he assuredly should have fainted if he had seen the patient bled.

Owing to my father's power of winning confidence, many patients, especially ladies, consulted him when suffering from any misery, as a sort of Father-Confessor. He told me that they always began by complaining in a vague manner about their health, and by practice he soon guessed what was really the matter. He then suggested that they had been suffering in their minds, and now they would pour out their troubles, and he heard nothing more about the body. Family quarrels were a common subject. When gentlemen complained to him about their wives, and the quarrel seemed serious, my Father advised them to act in the following manner; and his advice always succeeded, if the gentleman followed it to the letter, which was not always the case. The husband was to say to his wife that he was very sorry that they could not live happily together,—that he felt sure that she would be happier if separated from him— that he did not blame her in the least (this was the point on which the man oftenest failed),—that he would not blame her to any of her relations or friends,—and lastly that he would settle on her as large a provision as he could afford. She was then asked to deliberate on this proposal. As no fault had been found, her temper was unruffled, and she soon felt what an awkward position she would be in, with no accusation to rebut, and with her husband and not herself proposing a separation. Invariably the lady begged her husband not to think of separation, and usually behaved much better ever afterwards.

Owing to my father's skill in winning confidence he received many strange confessions of misery and guilt. He often remarked how many miserable wives he had known. In several instances husbands and wives had gone on pretty well together for between 20 and 30 years, and then hated each other bitterly: this he attributed to their having lost a common bond in their young children having grown up.

But the most remarkable power which my father possessed was that of reading the characters, and even the thoughts of those whom he saw even for a short time. We had many instances of this power, some of which seemed almost supernatural. It saved my father from ever making (with one exception, and the character of this man was soon discovered) an unworthy friend. A strange clergyman came to Shrewsbury, and seemed to be a rich man; everybody called on him and he was invited to many houses. My father called, and on his return home told my sisters on no account to invite him or his family to our house; for he felt sure that the man was not to be trusted. After a few months he suddenly bolted, being heavily in debt, and was found out to be little better than an habitual swindler. Here is a case of trust-fulness, which not many men would have ventured on. An Irish gentleman, a complete stranger, called on my father one day, and said that he had lost his purse, and that it would be a serious inconvenience to him to wait in Shrewsbury until he could receive a remittance from Ireland. He then asked my father to lend him 20 £, which was immediately done, as my father felt certain that the story was a true one. As soon as a letter could arrive from Ireland, one came with the most profuse thanks, and enclosing, as he said, a 20*l*. Bank of England note; but no note was enclosed. I asked my father whether this did not stagger him, but he answered 'not in the least'. On the next day another letter came with many apologies for having forgotten (like a true Irishman) to put the note into his letter of the day before.

A connection of my Father's consulted him about his son who was strangely idle and would settle to no work. My father said 'I believe that the foolish young man thinks that I shall bequeath him a large sum of money. Tell him that I have declared to you that I shall not leave him a penny.' The Father of the youth owned with shame that this preposterous idea had taken possession of his son's mind; and he asked my father how he could possibly have discovered it, but my father said he did not in the least know.

The Earl of —— brought his nephew, who was insane but quite gentle, to my father; and the young man's insanity led him to accuse himself of all the crimes under heaven. When my father afterwards talked about the case with the uncle, he said 'I am sure that your nephew is really guilty of . . . a heinous crime.' Whereupon the Earl of —— exclaimed, 'Good God, Dr. Darwin, who told you; we thought that no human being knew the fact except ourselves!' My father told me the story many years after the event, and I asked him how he distinguished the true from the false self-accusations; and it was very characteristic of my father that he said he could not explain how it was.

The following story shows what good guesses my father could make. Lord Sherburn,[1] afterwards the first Marquis of Landsdowne, was famous (as Macaulay somewhere remarks) for his knowledge of the affairs of Europe, on which he greatly prided himself. He consulted my father medically, and afterwards harangued him on the state of Holland. My father had studied medicine at Leyden, and one day went a long walk into the country with a friend, who took him to the house of a clergyman (we will say the Rev. Mr. A., for I have forgotten his name), who had married an Englishwoman. My father was very hungry, and there was little for luncheon except cheese, which he could never eat. The old lady was surprised and grieved at this, and assured my father that it was an excellent cheese and had been sent her from Bowood, the seat of L: Sherburn. My father wondered why a cheese should have been sent her from

Bowood, but thought nothing more about it, until it flashed across his mind many years afterwards whilst L: Sherburn was talking about Holland. So he answered, 'I should think from what I saw of the Rev. Mr. A. that he was a very able man and well acquainted with the state of Holland.' My father saw that the Earl, who immediately changed the conversation, was much startled. On the next morning my father received a note from the Earl, saying that he had delayed starting on his journey, and wished particularly to see my father. When he called the Earl said, 'Dr. Darwin, it is of the utmost importance to me and to the Rev. Mr. A. to learn how you have discovered that he is the source of my information about Holland.' So my father had to explain the state of the case, and he supposed that L.ᵈ Sherburn was much struck with his diplomatic skill in guessing, for during many years afterwards he received many kind messages from him through various friends. I think that he must have told the story to his children; for Sir C. Lyell asked me many years ago why the Marquis of Lansdown (the son or grandson of the first marquis) felt so much interest about me, whom he had never seen, and my family. When 40 new members (the 40 thieves as they were then called) were added to the Athenaeum Club, there was much canvassing to be one of them; and without my having asked anyone, L.ᵈ Lansdown proposed me and got me elected. If I am right in my supposition, it was a queer concatenation of events that my father not eating cheese half-a-century before in Holland led to my election as a member of the Athenaeum.

Early in life my father occasionally wrote down a short account of some curious events and conversations, which are enclosed in a separate envelope.

The sharpness of his observation led him to predict with remarkable skill the course of any illness, and he suggested endless small details of relief. I was told that a young Doctor in Shrewsbury who disliked my father, used to say that he was wholly unscientific, but owned that his power of predicting the end of an illness was unparalleled. Formerly when he thought that I should be a doctor, he talked much to me about his patients. In the old days the practice of bleeding largely was universal, but my father maintained that far more evil was thus caused than good done; and he advised me, if ever I was myself ill not to allow any doctor to take from me more than an extremely small quantity of blood. Long before typhoid fever was recognised as distinct, my father told me that two utterly distinct kinds of illness were confounded under the name of typhus fever. He was vehement against drinking, and was convinced of both the direct and inherited evil effects of alcohol, when habitually taken even in moderate quantity, in a very large majority of cases. But he admitted and advanced instances of certain persons, who could drink largely during their whole lives, without apparently suffering any evil effects; and he believed that he could often before-hand tell who would not thus suffer. He himself never drank a drop of any alcoholic fluid. This remark reminds me of a case showing how a witness under the most favourable circumstances may be wholly mistaken. A gentleman-farmer was strongly urged by my father not to drink, and was encouraged by being told that he himself never touched any spirituous liquor. Whereupon the gentleman said, 'Come, come, Doctor, that won't do, — though it is very kind of you to say so for my sake, — for I know that you take a very large glass of hot gin and water every evening after your dinner.' So my father asked him how he knew this. The man answered, 'My cook was your kitchen-maid for 2 or 3 years, and she saw the butler every day prepare and take to you the gin and water.' The explanation was that my father had the odd habit of drinking hot water in a very tall and large glass after his dinner; and the butler used first to put some cold water in the glass, which the girl mistook for gin, and then filled it up with boiling water from the kitchen-boiler.

My father used to tell me many little things which he had found useful in his medical practice. Thus ladies often cried much while telling him their troubles, and thus caused much loss of his precious time. He soon found that begging them to command and restrain themselves, always made them weep the more, so that afterwards he always encouraged them to go on crying, saying that this would relieve them more than anything else, with the invariable result that they soon ceased to cry, and he could hear what they had to say and give his advice. When patients, who were very ill, craved for some strange and unnatural food, my father asked them what had put such an idea into their heads: if they answered that they did not know, he would allow them to try the food and often with success, as he trusted to their having a kind of instinctive desire; but if they answered that they had heard that the food in question had done good to some one else, he firmly refused his assent.

He gave one day an odd little specimen of human nature. When a very young man he was called in to consult with the family physician in the case of a gentleman of much distinction in Shropshire. The old doctor told the wife that the illness was of such a nature that it must end fatally. My father took a different view and maintained that the gentleman would recover; he was proved quite wrong in all respects, (I think by autopsy) and he owned his error. He was then convinced that he should never again be consulted by this family; but after a few months the widow sent for him, having dismissed the old family doctor. My father was so much surprised at this, that he asked a friend of the widow to find out why he was again consulted. The widow answered her friend, that she would never again see that odious old doctor who said from the first that her husband would die, while Dr. Darwin always maintained that he would recover! In another case my father told a lady that her husband would certainly die. Some months afterward he saw the widow who was a very sensible woman, and she said, 'You are a very young man, and allow me to advise you always to give, as long as you possibly can, hope to any near relation nursing a patient. You made me despair, and from that moment I lost strength.' My father said that he had often since seen the paramount importance for the sake of the patient, of keeping up the hope and with it the strength of the nurse in charge. This he sometimes found it difficult to do compatibly with truth. One old gentleman, however, Mr. Pemberton, caused him no such perplexity. He was sent for by Mr. Pemberton, who said, 'From all that I have seen and heard of you, I believe you are the sort of man who will speak the truth, and if I ask you will tell me when I am dying. Now I much desire that you should attend me if you will promise, whatever I may say, always to declare that I am not going to die.' My father acquiesced on this understanding that his words should in fact have no meaning.

My father possessed an extraordinary memory, especially for dates, so that he knew when he was very old the day of the birth, marriage and death of a multitude of persons in Shropshire; and he once told me that this power annoyed him, for if he once heard a date he could not forget it; and thus the deaths of many friends were often recalled to his mind. Owing to his strong memory he knew an extraordinary number of curious stories, which he liked to tell as he was a great talker. He was generally in high spirits, and laughed and joked with everyone, often with his servants with the utmost freedom; yet he had the art of making everyone obey him to the letter. Many persons were much afraid of him. I remember my father telling us one day with a laugh that several persons had asked him whether Miss Pigott (a grand old lady in Shropshire) had called on him, so that at last he enquired why they asked him, and was told that Miss Pigott, whom my father had somehow mortally offended, was telling everybody that she would call and tell 'that fat old doctor very plainly what she thought of him.' She had already called, but her courage had failed, and no one could have been more courteous and friendly.—As a boy I went to stay at the house of Major B., whose wife was insane; and the poor creature, as soon as she saw me, was in the most abject state of terror that I ever saw, weeping bitterly and asking me over and over again, 'Is your father coming?'; but was soon pacified. On my return home I asked my father why she was so frightened, and he answered he [was] very glad to hear it, as he had frightened her on purpose, feeling sure that she could be kept in safety and much happier without any restraint, if her husband could influence her, whenever she became at all violent, by proposing to send for Dr. Darwin; and these words succeeded perfectly during the rest of her long life.

My father was very sensitive so that many small events annoyed or pained him much. I once asked him when he was old and could not walk, why he did not drive out for exercise; and he answered, 'Every road out of Shrewsbury is associated in my mind with some painful event.' Yet he was generally in high spirits. He was easily made very angry, but as his kindness was unbounded, he was widely and deeply loved.

He was a cautious and good man of business, so that he hardly ever lost money by any investment, and left to his children a very large property. I remember a story, showing how easily utterly false beliefs originate and spread. Mr. E., a squire of one of the oldest families in Shropshire and head partner in a Bank, committed suicide. My father was sent for as a matter of form, and found him dead. I may mention by the way to show how matters were managed in those old days, that because Mr. E. was a rather great man and universally respected, no inquest was held over his body. My father in returning home thought it proper to call at the Bank (where he had an account) to tell the managing partner of the event, as it was not improbable it would cause a run on the bank. Well the story was spread far and wide, that my father went into the bank, drew out all his money, left the bank, came back again and said, 'I may just tell you that Mr. E. has killed himself,' and then departed. It seems that it was then a common belief that money withdrawn from a bank was not safe, until the person had passed out through the door of the bank. My father did not hear this story till some little time afterwards, when the managing partner said that he had departed from his invariable rule of never allowing any one to see the account of another man, by having shown the ledger with my father's account to several persons, as this proved that my father had not drawn out a penny on that day. It would have been dishonourable in my father to have used his professional knowledge for his private advantage. Nevertheless the supposed act was greatly admired by some persons; and many years afterwards a gentleman remarked, 'Ah Doctor what a splendid man of business you were in so cleverly getting all your money safe out of that bank.'—

My father's mind was not scientific, and he did not try to generalise his knowledge under general laws; yet he formed a theory for almost everything which occurred. I do not think that I gained much from him intellectually; but his example ought to have been of much moral service to all his children. One of his golden rules (a hard one to follow) was 'Never become the friend of any one whom you cannot respect.'

With respect to my father's father,[1] the author of the Botanic Garden etc., I have put together all the facts which I could collect in his published Life.

Having said this much about my father, I will add a few words about my brother and sisters.

My brother Erasmus possessed a remarkably clear mind, with extensive and diversified tastes and knowledge in literature, art, and even in science. For a short time he collected and dried plants, and during a somewhat longer time experimented in chemistry. He was extremely agreeable, and his wit often reminded me of that in the letters and works of Charles Lamb. He was very kind-hearted; but his health from his boyhood had been weak, and as a consequence he failed in energy. His spirits were not high, sometimes low, more especially during early and middle man-hood. He read much, even whilst a boy, and at school encouraged me to read, lending me books. Our minds and tastes were, however, so different, that I do not think that I owe much to him intellectually, nor to my four sisters who possessed very different characters, and some of them had strongly marked characters. All were extremely kind and affectionate towards me during their whole lives. I am inclined to agree with Francis Galton in believing that education and environment produce only a small effect on the mind of any one, and that most of our qualities are innate.

The above sketch of my brother's character was written before that which was published in Carlyle's Remembrances,[2] and which appears to me to have little truth and no merit.

Looking back as well as I can at my character during my school-life, the only qualities which at this period promised well for the future, were, that I had strong and diversified tastes, much zeal for whatever interested me, and a keen pleasure in understanding any

Dr Robert Darwin
Contemporary silhouette c. 1826

Erasmus Darwin

Emma Darwin, née Wedgwood

Charles Darwin, c. 1850

complex subject or thing. I was taught Euclid by a private tutor, and I distinctly remember the intense satisfaction which the clear geometrical proofs gave me. I remember with equal distinctness the delight which my uncle[1] gave me (the father of Francis Galton) by explaining the principle of the vernier to a barometer. With respect to diversified tastes, independently of science, I was fond of reading various books, and I used to sit for hours reading the historical plays of Shakespeare, generally in an old window in the thick walls of the school. I read also other poetry, such as the recently published poems of Byron, Scott, Thompson's Seasons. I mention this because later in life I wholly lost, to my great regret, all pleasure from poetry of any kind, including Shakespeare. In connection with pleasure from poetry I may add that in 1822 a vivid delight in scenery was first awakened in my mind, during a riding tour on the borders of Wales, and which has lasted longer than any other aesthetic pleasure.

Early in my school days a boy had a copy of the Wonders of the World, which I often read and disputed with other boys about the veracity of some of the statements; and I believe this book first gave me a wish to travel in remote countries which was ultimately fulfilled by the voyage of the Beagle. In the latter part of my school life I became passionately fond of shooting, and I do not believe that any one could have shown more zeal for the most holy cause than I did for shooting birds. How well I remember killing my first snipe, and my excitement was so great that I had much difficulty in reloading my gun from the trembling of my hands. This taste long continued and I became a very good shot. When at Cambridge I used to practice throwing up my gun to my shoulder before a looking glass to see that I threw it up straight. Another and better plan was to get a friend to wave about a lighted candle and then to fire at it with a cap on the nipple, and if the aim was accurate the little puff of air would blow out the candle. The explosion of the cap caused a sharp crack, and I was told that the Tutor of the College remarked, 'What an extraordinary thing it is, Mr. Darwin seems to spend hours in cracking a horsewhip in his room, for I often hear the crack when I pass under his windows.'

I had many friends amongst the school-boys, whom I loved dearly, and I think that my disposition was then very affectionate. Some of these boys were rather clever, but I may add on the principle of 'noscitur a socio' that not one of them ever became in the least distinguished.

With respect to science, I continued collecting minerals with much zeal, but quite unscientifically—all that I cared for was a new *named* mineral, and I hardly attempted to classify them. I must have observed insects with some little care, for when 10 years old (1819) I went for 3 weeks to Plas Edwards on the sea-coast in Wales, I was very much interested and surprised at seeing a large black and scarlet Hemipterous insect, many moths (Zygæna), and a Cicindela, which are not found in Shropshire. I almost made up my mind to begin collecting all the insects which I could find dead, for on consulting my sister I concluded that it was not right to kill insects for the sake of making a collection. From reading White's Selborne I took much pleasure in watching the habits of birds and even made notes on this subject. In my simplicity I remember wondering why every gentleman did not become an ornithologist.

Towards the close of my school-life, my brother worked hard at chemistry and made a fair laboratory with proper apparatus in the tool-house in the garden, and I was allowed to aid him as a servant in most of his experiments. He made all the gases and many compounds, and I read with care several books on chemistry, such as Henry and Parkes'[1] Ch. Catechism. The subject interested me greatly, and we often used to go on working till rather late at night. This was the best part of my education at school, for it showed me practically the meaning of experimental science. The fact that we worked at chemistry somehow got known at school, and as it was an unprecedented fact, I was nicknamed 'Gas'. I was also once publicly rebuked by the head-master, Dr. Butler, for thus wasting my time over such useless subjects; and he called me very unjustly a 'poco curante,' and as I did not understand what he meant it seemed to me a fearful reproach.

As I was doing no good at school, my father wisely took me

away at a rather earlier age than usual, and sent me (October 1825) to Edinburgh University with my brother, where I staid for two years or sessions. My brother was completing his medical studies, though I do not believe he ever really intended to practice, and I was sent there to commence them. But soon after this period I became convinced from various small circumstances that my Father would leave me property enough to subsist on with some comfort, though I never imagined that I should be so rich a man as I am; but my belief was sufficient to check any strenuous effort to learn medicine.

The instruction at Edinburgh was altogether by lectures, and these were intolerably dull, with the exception of those in chemistry by Hope; but to my mind there are no advantages and many disadvantages in lectures compared with reading. Dr. Duncan's lectures on Materia Medica at 8 o'clock on a winter's morning are something fearful to remember. Dr. Munro made his lectures on human anatomy as dull, as he was himself, and the subject disgusted me. It has proved one of the greatest evils in my life that I was not urged to practice dissection, for I should soon have got over my disgust; and the practice would have been invaluable for all my future work. This has been an irremediable evil, as well as my incapacity to draw. I also attended regularly the clinical wards in the Hospital. Some of the cases distressed me a good deal, and I still have vivid pictures before me of some of them; but I was not so foolish as to allow this to lessen my attendance. I cannot understand why this part of my medical course did not interest me in a greater degree; for during the summer before coming to Edinburgh I began attending some of the poor people, chiefly children and women, in Shrewsbury: I wrote down as full an account as I could of the cases with all the symptoms, and read them aloud to my Father, who suggested further enquiries, and advised me what medicines to give, which I made up myself. At one time I had at least a dozen patients, and I felt a keen interest in the work. My Father, who was by far the best judge of character whom I ever knew, declared that I should make a successful physician,—meaning by this one who got many patients.

He maintained that the chief element of success was exciting confidence; but what he saw in me which convinced him that I should create confidence I know not. I also attended on two occasions the operating theatre in the Hospital at Edinburgh, and saw two very bad operations, one on a child, but I rushed away before they were completed. Nor did I ever attend again, for hardly any inducement would have been strong enough to make me do so; this being long before the blessed days of chloroform. The two cases fairly haunted me for many a long year.

My Brother staid only one year at the University, so that during the second year I was left to my own resources; and this was an advantage, for I became well acquainted with several young men fond of natural science. One of these was Ainsworth, who afterwards published his travels in Assyria: he was a Wernerian[1] geologist and knew a little about many subjects, but was superficial and very glib with his tongue. Dr. Coldstream was a very different young man, prim, formal, highly religious and most kind-hearted: he afterwards published some good zoological articles. A third young man was Hardie, who would I think have made a good botanist, but died early in India. Lastly Dr. Grant, my senior by several years, but how I became acquainted with him I cannot remember: he published some first-rate zoological papers, but after coming to London as Professor in University College he did nothing more in science, a fact which has always been inexplicable to me. I knew him well; he was dry and formal in manner, but with much enthusiasm beneath this outer crust. He one day when we were walking together burst forth in high admiration of Lamarck and his views on evolution. I listened in silent astonishment, and as far as I can judge without any effect on my mind. I had previously read the Zoönomia[2] of my grandfather, in which similar views are maintained, but without producing any effect on me. Nevertheless it is probable that the hearing rather early in life such views maintained and praised may have favoured my upholding them under a different form in my Origin of Species. At this time I admired greatly the Zoönomia; but on reading it a second time after an interval of 10 or 15 years, I was much disappointed, the proportion of speculation being so large to the facts given.

Drs. Grant and Coldstream attended much to marine zoology, and I often accompanied the former to collect animals in the tidal pools, which I dissected as well as I could. I also became friends with some of the Newhaven fishermen, and sometimes accompanied them when they trawled for oysters, and thus got many specimens. But from not having had any regular practice in dissection and from possessing only a wretched microscope my attempts were very poor. Nevertheless I made one interesting little discovery, and read about the beginning of the year 1826, a short paper on the subject before the Plinian Socy. This was that the so-called ova of Flustra had the power of independent movement by means of cilia, and were in fact larvæ. In another short paper I showed that little globular bodies, which had been supposed to be the young state of Fucus loreus were the egg-cases of the worm-like Pontobdella muricata.

The Plinian Society was encouraged and I believe founded by Professor Jameson: it consisted of students and met in an underground room in the University for the sake of reading papers on natural science and discussing them. I used regularly to attend, and the meetings had a good effect on me in stimulating my zeal and giving me new congenial acquaintances. One evening a poor young man got up and after stammering for a prodigious length of time, blushing crimson, he at last slowly got out the words, 'Mr. President I have forgotten what I was going to say.' The poor fellow looked quite overwhelmed and all the members were so surprised that no one could think of a word to say to cover his confusion. The papers which were read to our little Society, were not printed, so that I had not the satisfaction of seeing my paper in print; but I believe Dr. Grant noticed my small discovery in his excellent memoir on Flustra.

I was also a member of the Royal Medical Soc.ʸ and attended pretty regularly, but as the subjects were exclusively medical, I did not much care about them. Much rubbish was talked there, but there were some good speakers, of whom the best was the present Sir J. Kay Shuttleworth. Dr. Grant took me occasionally to the meetings of the Wernerian Soc.ʸ, where various papers on natural history were read, discussed, and afterwards published in the Transactions. I heard Audubon deliver there some interesting discourses on the habits of N. American birds, sneering somewhat unjustly at Waterton. By the way a negro lived in Edinburgh, who had travelled with Waterton, and gained his livelihood by stuffing birds, which he did excellently: he gave me lessons for payment, and I used often to sit with him, for he was a very pleasant and intelligent man.

Mr. Leonard Horner also took me once to a meeting of the Royal Society of Edinburgh, where I saw Sir Walter Scott in the chair as President, and he apologised to the meeting as not feeling fitted for such a position. I looked at him and at the whole scene with some awe and reverence; and I think it was owing to this visit during my youth and to my having attended the R. Medical Soc.ʸ, that I felt the honour of being elected a few years ago an Honorary Member of both these Societies, more than any other similar honour. If I had been told at that time that I should one day have been thus honoured, I declare that I should have thought it as ridiculous and improbable, as if I had been told that I should be elected King of England.

During my second year in Edinburgh I attended Jameson's lectures on Geology and Zoology, but they were incredibly dull. The sole effect they produced on me was the determination never as long as I lived to read a book on geology or in any way to study the science. Yet I feel sure that I was prepared for a philosophical treatment of the subject; for an old Mr. Cotton in Shropshire who knew a good deal about rocks had pointed out to me, 2 or 3 years previously, a well-known large erratic boulder in the town of Shrewsbury called the bell-stone; he told me that there was no rock of the same kind nearer than Cumberland or Scotland, and he solemnly assured me that the world would come to an end before anyone would be able to explain how this stone came where it now lay. This produced a deep impression on me and I meditated over this wonderful stone. So that I felt the keenest delight when I first read of the action of icebergs in transporting boulders, and I gloried in the progress of geology.

Equally striking is the fact that I though now only 67 years old heard Prof. Jameson in a field lecture at Salisbury Craigs discoursing on a trap-dyke, with amygdaloidal margins and the strata indurated on each side, with volcanic rocks all around us, and say that it was a fissure filled with sediment from above, adding with a sneer that there were men who maintained that it had been injected from beneath in a molten condition. When I think of this lecture, I do not wonder that I determined never to attend to Geology.

From attending Jameson's lectures, I became acquainted with the curator of the Museum, Mr. Macgillivray, who afterwards published a large and excellent book on the birds of Scotland. He had not much of the appearance or manners of the gentleman, but I had much interesting natural history talk with him, and he was very kind to me. He gave me some rare shells, for I at that time collected marine mollusca, but with no great zeal.

My summer vacations during these two years were wholly given up to amusements, though I always had some book in hand which I read with interest. During the summer of 1826, I took a long walking tour with two friends with knapsacks on our backs through North Wales. We walked 30 miles most days, including one day the ascent of Snowdon. I also went with my sister Caroline a riding tour in North Wales, a servant with saddle-bags carrying our clothes. The autumns were devoted to shooting, chiefly at Mr. Owens[1] at Woodhouse, and at my Uncle Jos'[2] at Maer. My zeal was so great that I used to place my shooting boots open by my bed side, when I went to bed, so as not to lose half-a-minute in putting them on in the morning; and on one occasion I reached a distant part of the Maer Estate on the 20th of August for black-game shooting before I could see: I then toiled on with the gamekeeper the whole day through thick heath and young Scotch-firs. I kept an exact record of every bird which I shot throughout the whole season. One day when shooting at Woodhouse with Capt. Owen the eldest son and Major Hill, his cousin, afterwards Ld. Berwick, both of whom I liked very much, I thought myself shamefully used, for every time after I had fired and thought that I had killed a bird, one of the two acted as if loading his gun and cried out, 'You must not count that bird, for I fired at the same time,' and the gamekeeper perceiving the joke backed them up. After some hours they told me the joke, but it was no joke to me for I had shot a large number of birds, but did not know how many and could not add them to my list, which I used to do by making a knot to a piece of string, tied to a button-hole. This my wicked friends had perceived.

How I did enjoy shooting, but I think that I must have been half-consciously ashamed of my zeal, for I tried to persuade myself that shooting was almost an intellectual employment; it required so much skill to judge where to find most game and to hunt the dogs well.

One of my autumnal visits to Maer in 1827 was memorable from meeting there Sir J. Mackintosh, who was the best converser I ever listened to. I heard afterward with a glow of pride that he had said, 'There is something in that young man which interests me.' This must have been chiefly due to his perceiving that I listened with much interest to everything which he said, for I was as ignorant as a pig about his subjects of history, politicks and moral philosophy. To hear of praise from an eminent person, though no doubt apt or certain to excite vanity, is, I think, good for a young man, as it helps to keep him in the right course.

My visits to Maer during these two and the three succeeding years were quite delightful, independently of the autumnal shooting. Life there was perfectly free; the country was very pleasant for walking or riding; and in the evening there was much very agreeable conversation, not so personal as it generally is in large family parties, together with music. In the summer the whole family used often to sit on the steps of the old portico, with the flower-garden in front, and with the steep wooded bank, opposite to the house, reflected in the lake, with here and there a fish rising or a water-bird paddling about. Nothing has left a more vivid picture on my mind than those evenings at Maer. I was also attached to and greatly revered my Uncle Jos: he was silent and reserved so as to be a rather awful man; but he sometimes talked openly with me. He was the very type of an upright man with the clearest judgment. I do not believe that any power on earth could have made him swerve an inch from what he considered the right course. I used to apply to him in my mind, the well-known ode of Horace, now forgotten by me, in which the words 'nec vultus tyranni &c.'[1] come in.

Cambridge 1828–1831

AFTER having spent two sessions in Edinburgh, my Father perceived or he heard from my sisters that I did not like the thought of being a physician, so he proposed that I should become a clergyman. He was very properly vehement against my turning an idle sporting man, which then seemed my probable destination. I asked for some time to consider, as from what little I had heard and thought on the subject I had scruples about declaring my belief in all the dogmas of the Church of England; though otherwise I liked the thought of being a country clergyman. Accordingly I read with care Pearson on the Creeds[2] and a few other books on divinity; and as I did not then in the least doubt the strict and literal truth of every word in the Bible, I soon persuaded myself that our Creed must be fully accepted. It never struck me how illogical it was to say that I believed in what I could not understand and what is in fact unintelligible. I might have said with entire truth that I had no wish to dispute any dogma; but I never was such a fool as to feel and say 'credo quia incredibile'.

Considering how fiercely I have been attacked by the orthodox, it seems ludicrous that I once intended to be a clergyman. Nor was this intention and my Father's wish ever formally given up, but died a natural death when on leaving Cambridge I joined the Beagle as Naturalist. If the phrenologists are to be trusted, I was well fitted in one respect to be a clergyman. A few years ago the Secretaries of a German psychological Soc.ᵞ asked me earnestly by letter for a photograph of myself; and some time afterwards I received the Proceedings of one of the meetings, in which it seemed that the shape of my head had been the subject of a public discussion, and one of the speakers declared that I had the bump of Reverence developed enough for ten Priests.

As it was decided that I should be a clergyman, it was necessary that I should go to one of the English Universities and take a degree; but as I had never opened a classical book since leaving school, I found to my dismay that in the two intervening years I had actually forgotten, incredible as it may appear, almost everything which I had learnt even to some few of the Greek letters. I did not therefore proceed to Cambridge at the usual time in October, but worked with a private tutor in Shrewsbury and went to Cambridge after the Christmas vacation, early in 1828. I soon recovered my school standard of knowledge, and could translate easy Greek books, such as Homer and the Greek Testament with moderate facility.

During the three years which I spent at Cambridge my time was wasted, as far as the academical studies were concerned, as completely as at Edinburgh and at school. I attempted mathematicks, and even went during the summer of 1828 with a private tutor (a very dull man) to Barmouth, but I got on very slowly. The work was repugnant to me, chiefly from my not being able to see any meaning in the early steps in algebra. This impatience was very foolish, and in after years I have deeply regretted that I did not proceed far enough at least to understand something of the great leading principles of mathematicks; for men thus endowed seem to have an extra sense. But I do not believe that I should ever have succeeded beyond a very low grade. With respect to classics I did nothing except attend a few compulsory college lectures, and the attendance was almost nominal. In my second year I had to work for a month or two to pass the Little Go, which I did easily. Again in my last year I worked with some earnestness for my final degree of B.A., and brushed up my Classics together with a little algebra and Euclid, which latter gave me much pleasure as it did whilst at school. In order to pass the B.A. examination it was, also, necessary to get up Paley's Evidences of Christianity and his Moral Philosophy.[1] This was done in a thorough manner, and I am convinced that I could have written out the whole of the Evidences with perfect correctness, but not of course in the clear language of Paley. The logic of this book, and as I may add of his Natural Theology gave me as much delight as did Euclid. The careful study of these works, without attempting to learn any part by rote, was the only part of the Academical Course which as I then felt and as I still believe, was of the least use to me in the education of my mind. I did not at that time trouble myself about Paley's premises; and taking these on trust I was charmed and convinced by the long line of argumentation. By answering well the examination questions in Paley, by doing Euclid well, and by not failing miserably in Classics, I gained a good place amongst the οἱ πολλοί, or crowd of men who do not go in for honours. Oddly enough I cannot remember[1] how high I stood, and my memory fluctuates between the fifth, tenth or twelfth name on the list.

Public lectures on several branches were given in the University, attendance being quite voluntary; but I was so sickened with lectures at Edinburgh that I did not even attend Sedgwick's eloquent and interesting lectures. Had I done so I should probably have become a geologist earlier than I did. I attended, however, Henslow's[2] lectures on Botany, and liked them much for their extreme clearness, and the admirable illustrations; but I did not study botany. Henslow used to take his pupils, including several of the older members of the University, field excursions, on foot, or in coaches to distant places, or in a barge down the river, and lectured on the rarer plants or animals which were observed. These excursions were delightful.

Although as we shall presently see there were some redeeming features in my life at Cambridge, my time was sadly wasted there and worse than wasted. From my passion for shooting and for hunting and when this failed for riding across country I got into a sporting set, including some dissipated, low-minded young men. We used often to dine together in the evening, though these dinners often included men of a higher stamp, and we sometimes drank too much, with jolly singing and playing at cards afterwards. I know that I ought to feel ashamed of days and evenings thus spent, but as some of my friends were very pleasant, and we were all in the highest spirits, I cannot help looking back to these times with much pleasure.

But I am glad to think that I had many other friends of a widely different nature. I was very intimate with Whitley, who was afterwards Senior Wrangler, and we used continually to take long walks together. He inoculated me with a taste for pictures and good engravings, of which I bought some. I frequently went to the Fitz-william Gallery, and my taste must have been fairly good, for I certainly admired the best pictures, which I discussed with the old curator. I read also with much interest Sir J. Reynolds' book. This taste, though not natural to me, lasted for several years and many of the pictures in the National Gallery in London gave me much pleasure; that of Sebastian del Piombo exciting in me a sense of sublimity.

I also got into a musical set, I believe by means of my warm-hearted friend, Herbert, who took a high wrangler's degree. From associating with these men and hearing them play, I acquired a strong taste for music, and used very often to time my walks so as to hear on week-days the anthem in King's College Chapel. This gave me intense pleasure, so that my back-bone would sometimes shiver. I am sure that there was no affectation or mere imitation in this taste, for I used generally to go by myself to Kings College, and I sometimes hired the chorister boys to sing in my rooms. Nevertheless I am so utterly destitute of an ear, that I cannot perceive a discord or keep time and hum a tune correctly; and it is a mystery how I could possibly have derived pleasure from music.

My musical friends soon perceived my state, and sometimes amused themselves by making me pass an examination, which consisted of ascertaining how many tunes I could recognise, when they were played rather more quickly or slowly than usual. 'God save the King' when thus played was a sore puzzle. There was another man with almost as bad an ear as I had, and strange to say he played a little on the flute. Once I had the triumph of beating him in one of our musical examinations.

But no pursuit at Cambridge was followed with nearly so much eagerness or gave me so much pleasure as collecting beetles. It was the mere passion for collecting, for I did not dissect them and rarely compared their external characters with published descriptions, but got them named anyhow. I will give a proof of my zeal: one day on tearing off some old bark, I saw two rare beetles and seized one in each hand; then I saw a third and new kind, which I could not bear to lose, so that I popped the one which I held in my right hand into my mouth. Alas it ejected some intensely acrid fluid, which burnt my tongue so that I was forced to spit the beetle out, which was lost, as well as the third one. I was very successful in collecting and invented two new methods; I employed a labourer to scrape during the winter moss off old trees and place [it] in a large bag, and likewise to collect the rubbish at the bottom of the barges in which reeds are brought from the fens, and thus I got some very rare species. No poet ever felt more delight at seeing his first poem published than I did at seeing in Stephen's 'Illustrations of British Insects' the magic words 'captured by C. Darwin, Esq.' I was introduced to Entomology by my second-cousin, W. Darwin Fox, a clever and most pleasant man, who was then at Christ College and with whom I became extremely intimate. Afterwards I became well acquainted with and went out collecting with Albert Way of Trinity, who in after years became a well-known archaeologist; also with H. Thompson of the same College, afterwards a leading agriculturist, chairman of a great Railway and member of parliament. It seems therefore that a taste for collecting beetles is some indication of future success in life!

I am surprised what an indelible impression many of the beetles which I caught at Cambridge have left on my mind. I can remember the exact appearance of certain posts, old trees and banks where I made a good capture. The pretty Panagæus crux-major was a treasure in those days, and here at Down I saw a beetle running across a walk, and on picking it up instantly perceived that it differed slightly from P. crux-major, and it turned out to be P. quadripunctatus, which is only a variety or closely allied species differing from it very slightly in outline. I had never seen in those old days Licinus alive, which to an uneducated eye hardly differs from many other black Carabidous beetles; but my sons found here a specimen and I instantly recognised that it was new to me; yet I had not looked at a British beetle for the last twenty years.

I have not as yet mentioned a circumstance which influenced my whole career more than any other. This was my friendship with Prof. Henslow. Before coming up to Cambridge, I had heard of him from my brother as a man who knew every branch of science, and I was accordingly prepared to reverence him. He kept open house once every week, where all undergraduates and several older members of the University, who were attached to science, used to meet in the evening. I soon got through Fox an invitation and went there regularly. Before long I became well acquainted with Henslow, and during the latter half of my time at Cambridge took long walks with him on most days; so that I was called by some of the dons 'the man who walks with Henslow'; and in the evening I was very often asked to join his family dinner. His knowledge was great in botany, entomology, chemistry, mineralogy and geology. His strongest taste was to draw conclusions from long-continued minute observations. His judgment was excellent, and his whole mind well-balanced; but I do not suppose that anyone would say that he possessed much original genius. He was deeply religious, and so orthodox that he told me one day, he should be grieved if a single word in the 39 Articles were altered. His moral qualities were in every way admirable. He was free from every tinge of vanity or other petty feeling; and I never saw a man who thought so little about himself or his own concerns. His temper was imperturbably good, with the most winning and courteous manners; yet, as I have seen, he could be roused by any bad action to the warmest indignation and prompt action. I once saw in his company in the streets of Cambridge, almost as horrid a scene, as could have been witnessed during the French Revolution. Two body-snatchers had been arrested and whilst being taken to prison had been torn from the constable by a crowd of the roughest men, who dragged them by their legs along the muddy and stony road. They were covered from head to foot with mud and their faces were bleeding either from having been kicked or from the stones; they looked like corpses, but the crowd was so dense that I got only a few momentary glimpses of the wretched creatures. Never in my life have I seen such wrath painted on a man's face, as was shown by Henslow at this horrid scene. He tried repeatedly to penetrate the mob; but it was simply impossible. He then rushed away to the mayor, telling me not to follow him, to get more policemen. I forget the issue, except that the two were got into the prison before being killed.

Henslow's benevolence was unbounded, as he proved by his many excellent schemes for his poor parishioners, when in after years he held the living of Hitcham. My intimacy with such a man ought to have been and I hope was an inestimable benefit. I cannot resist mentioning a trifling incident, which showed his kind consideration. Whilst examining some pollen-grains on a damp surface I saw the tubes exserted, and instantly rushed off to communicate my surprising discovery to him. Now I do not suppose any other Professor of Botany could have helped laughing at my coming in a hurry to make such a communication. But he agreed how interesting the phenomenon was and explained its meaning, but made me clearly understand how well it was known; so I left him not in the least mortified, but well pleased at having discovered for myself so remarkable a fact, but determined not to be in such a hurry again to communicate my discoveries.

Dr. Whewell was one of the older and distinguished men who sometimes visited Henslow, and on several occasions I walked home with him at night. Next to Sir J. Mackintosh he was the best converser on grave subjects to whom I ever listened. Leonard Jenyns, (grandson of the famous Soames Jenyns), who afterwards published some good essays in Natural History, often staid with Henslow, who was his brother-in-law. At first I disliked him from his somewhat grim and sarcastic expression; and it is not often that a first impression is lost; but I was completely mistaken and found him very kindhearted, pleasant and with a good stock of humour. I visited him at his parsonage on the borders of the Fens, and had many a good walk and talk with him about Natural History. I became also acquainted with several other men older than me, who did not care much about science, but were friends of Henslow. One was a Scotchman, brother of Sir Alexander Ramsay, and tutor of Jesus College; he was a delightful man, but did not live for many years. Another was Mr.

Dawes, afterwards Dean of Hereford and famous for his success in the education of the poor. These men and others of the same standing, together with Henslow used sometimes to take distant excursions into the country, which I was allowed to join and they were most agreeable.

Looking back, I infer that there must have been something in me a little superior to the common run of youths, otherwise the above-mentioned men, so much older than me and higher in academical position, would never have allowed me to associate with them. Certainly I was not aware of any such superiority, and I remember one of my sporting friends, Turner, who saw me at work on my beetles, saying that I should some day be a fellow of the Royal Society, and the notion seemed to me preposterous.

During my last year at Cambridge I read with care and profound interest Humboldt's Personal Narrative. This work and Sir J. Herschel's Introduction to the Study of Natural Philosophy stirred up in me a burning zeal to add even the most humble contribution to the noble structure of Natural Science. No one or a dozen other books influenced me nearly so much as these two. I copied out from Humboldt long passages about Teneriffe, and read them aloud on one of the above-mentioned excursions, to (I think) Henslow, Ramsay and Dawes; for on a previous occasion I had talked about the glories of Teneriffe and some of the party declared they would endeavour to go there; but I think that they were only half in earnest. I was, however, quite in earnest, and got an introduction to a merchant in London to enquire about ships; but the scheme was of course knocked on the head by the voyage of the Beagle.

My summer vacations were given up to collecting beetles, to some reading and short tours. In the autumn my whole time was devoted to shooting, chiefly at Woodhouse and Maer, and sometimes with young Eyton of Eyton. Upon the whole the three years which I spent at Cambridge were the most joyful in my happy life; for I was then in excellent health, and almost always in high spirits.

As I had at first come up to Cambridge at Christmas, I was forced to keep two terms after passing my final examination, at the com-

Alexander, Baron von Humboldt

Sir Charles Lyell

Sir John Herschel
Photograph by Julia Cameron

John Stevens Henslow

H.M.S. Beagle: water colour by Captain Owen Stanley, R.N.

mencement of 1831; and Henslow then persuaded me to begin the study of geology. Therefore on my return to Shropshire I examined sections and coloured a map of parts round Shrewsbury. Professor Sedgwick intended to visit N. Wales in the beginning of August to pursue his famous geological investigation amongst the older rocks, and Henslow asked him to allow me to accompany him. Accordingly he came and slept at my Father's house. A short conversation with him during this evening produced a strong impression on my mind. Whilst examining an old gravel pit near Shrewsbury a labourer told me that he had found in it, a large worn tropical Volute shell, such as may be seen on the chimney-pieces of cottages; and as he would not sell the shell I was convinced that he had really found it in the pit. I told Sedgwick of the fact, and he at once said (no doubt truly) that it must have been thrown away by some one into the pit; but then added, if really embedded there it would be the greatest misfortune to geology, as it would overthrow all that we know about the superficial deposits of the midland counties. These gravel-beds belonged in fact to the glacial period, and in after years I found in them broken arctic shells. But I was then utterly astonished at Sedgwick not being delighted at so wonderful a fact as a tropical shell being found near the surface in the middle of England. Nothing before had ever made me thoroughly realise, though I had read various scientific books, that science consists in grouping facts so that general laws or conclusions may be drawn from them.

Next morning we started for Llangollen, Conway, Bangor, and Capel Curig. This tour was of decided use in teaching me a little how to make out the geology of a country. Sedgwick often sent me on a line parallel to his, telling me to bring back specimens of the rocks and to mark the stratification on a map. I have little doubt that he did this for my good, as I was too ignorant to have aided him. On this tour I had a striking instance how easy it is to overlook phenomena, however conspicuous, before they have been observed by any one. We spent many hours in Cwm Idwall, examining all the rocks with extreme care, as Sedgwick was anxious to find fossils in them; but neither of us saw a trace of the wonderful glacial phenomena all around us; we did not notice the plainly scored rocks, the perched boulders, the lateral and terminal moraines. Yet these phenomena are so conspicuous, that as I declared in a paper published many years afterwards in the Philosophical Magazine,[1] a house burnt down by fire did not tell its story more plainly than did this valley. If it had still been filled by a glacier, the phenomena would have been less distinct than they now are.

At Capel-Curig I left Sedgwick and went in a straight line by compass and map across the mountains to Barmouth, never following any track unless it coincided with my course. I thus came on some strange wild places and enjoyed much this manner of travelling. I visited Barmouth to see some Cambridge friends who were reading there, and thence returned to Shrewsbury and to Maer for shooting; for at that time I should have thought myself mad to give up the first days of partridge-shooting for geology or any other science.

Voyage of the Beagle from Dec. 27 1831 to Oct. 2 1836

ON returning home from my short geological tour in N. Wales, I found a letter from Henslow, informing me that Captain Fitz Roy was willing to give up part of his own cabin to any young man who would volunteer to go with him without pay as naturalist to the Voyage of the Beagle. I have given as I believe in my M.S. Journal an account of all the circumstances which then occurred; I will here only say that I was instantly eager to accept the offer, but my Father strongly objected, adding the words fortunate for me,—'If you can find any man of common sense, who advises you to go, I will give my consent.' So I wrote that evening and refused the offer. On the next morning I went to Maer to be ready for September 1st, and whilst out shooting, my Uncle sent for me offering to drive me over to Shrewsbury and talk with my Father. As my Uncle thought it would be wise in me to accept the offer, and as my Father always maintained that he was one of the most sensible men in the world, he at once consented in the kindest manner. I had been rather extravagant at Cambridge and to console my Father said 'that I should be deuced

clever to spend more than my allowance whilst on board the Beagle';
but he answered with a smile, 'But they all tell me you are very
clever.'

Next day I started for Cambridge to see Henslow, and thence to
London to see Fitz Roy, and all was soon arranged. Afterwards on
becoming very intimate with Fitz Roy, I heard that I had run a very
narrow risk of being rejected, on account of the shape of my nose!
He was an ardent disciple of Lavater, and was convinced that he
could judge of a man's character by the outline of his features; and he
doubted whether anyone with my nose could possess sufficient energy
and determination for the voyage. But I think he was afterwards well-
satisfied that my nose had spoken falsely.

Fitz Roy's character was a singular one, with many very noble
features: he was devoted to his duty, generous to a fault, bold,
determined, indomitably energetic, and an ardent friend to all under
his sway. He would undertake any sort of trouble to assist those
whom he thought deserved assistance. He was a handsome man,
strikingly like a gentleman, with highly courteous manners, which
resembled those of his maternal uncle the famous Ld Castlereagh,
as I was told by the Minister at Rio. Nevertheless he must have
inherited much in his appearance from Charles II, for Dr. Wallich
gave me a collection of photographs, which he had made, and I was
struck with the resemblance of one to Fitz Roy; on looking at the
name I found it Ch. E. Sobieski Stuart, Count d'Albanie, an illegitimate descendant of this same monarch.

Fitz Roy's temper was a most unfortunate one, and this was shown
not only by passion but by fits of long-continued moroseness against
those who had offended him. His temper was usually worst in the
early morning, and with his eagle eye he could generally detect
something amiss about the ship, and was then unsparing in his blame.
The junior officers, when they relieved each other in the forenoon
used to ask 'whether much hot coffee had been served out this
morning,'—which meant how was the Captain's temper? He was
also somewhat suspicious and occasionally in very low spirits, on one
occasion bordering on insanity. He seemed to me often to fail in

sound judgment or common sense. He was extremely kind to me, but was a man very difficult to live with on the intimate terms which necessarily followed from our messing by ourselves in the same cabin. We had several quarrels; for when out of temper he was utterly unreasonable. For instance, early in the voyage at Bahia in Brazil he defended and praised slavery which I abominated, and told me that he had just visited a great slave-owner, who had called up many of his slaves and asked them whether they were happy, and whether they wished to be free, and all answered 'No'. I then asked him, perhaps with a sneer, whether he thought that the answers of slaves in the presence of their master was worth anything. This made him excessively angry, and he said, that as I doubted his word, we could not live any longer together. I thought that I should have been compelled to leave the ship; but as soon as the news spread, which it did quickly, as the Captain sent for the first Lieutenant to assuage his anger by abusing me, I was deeply gratified by receiving an invitation from all the gun-room officers to mess with them. But after a few hours Fitz Roy showed his usual magnanimity, by sending an officer to me with an apology and a request that I would continue to live with him. I remember another instance of his candour. At Plymouth, before we sailed, he was extremely angry with a dealer in crockery who refused to exchange some article purchased in his shop: the Captain asked the man the price of a very expensive set of china and said 'I should have purchased this, if you had not been so disobliging.' As I knew that the cabin was amply stocked with crockery, I doubted whether he had any such intention; and I must have shown my doubts in my face, for I said not a word. After leaving the shop he looked at me, saying You do not believe what I have said, and I was forced to own that it was so. He was silent for a few minutes, and then said You are right, and I acted wrongly in my anger at the blackguard.

At Conception in Chile, poor Fitz Roy was sadly overworked and in very low spirits; he complained bitterly to me that he must give a great party to all the inhabitants of the place. I remonstrated and said that I could see no such necessity on his part under the circumstances.

He then burst out into a fury, declaring that I was the sort of man who would receive any favours and make no return. I got up and left the cabin without saying a word, and returned to Conception, where I was then lodging. After a few days I came back to the ship, and was received by the Captain, as cordially as ever, for the storm had by that time quite blown over. The first Lieutenant,[1] however, said to me: 'Confound you, philosopher, I wish you would not quarrel with the skipper; the day you left the ship I was dead-tired (the ship was refitting) and he kept me walking the deck till midnight, abusing you all the time.' The difficulty of living on good terms with a Captain of a Man of War is much increased by its being almost mutinous to answer him, as one would answer anyone else; and by the awe in which he is held, or was held in my time, by all on board. I remember hearing a curious instance of this in the case of the Purser of the Adventure,—the ship which sailed with the Beagle during the first Voyage. The Purser was in a store in Rio de Janeiro, purchasing rum for the ship's company, and a little gentleman in plain clothes walked in. The Purser said to him, 'Now, Sir, be so kind as to taste this rum, and give me your opinion of it.' The gentleman did as he was asked, and soon left the store. The store-keeper then asked the Purser, whether he knew that he had been speaking to the Captain of a Line of Battle Ship which had just come into the harbour. The poor purser was struck dumb with horror; he let the glass of spirit drop from his hand on to the floor, and immediately went on board, and no persuasion, as an officer on the Adventure assured me, could make him go on shore again for fear of meeting the Captain after his dreadful act of familiarity.

I saw Fitz Roy only occasionally after our return home, for I was always afraid of unintentionally offending him, and did so once, almost beyond mutual reconciliation. He was afterward very indignant with me for having published so unorthodox a book (for he became very religious) as the Origin of Species. Towards the close of his life he was, as I fear, much impoverished, and this was largely due to his generosity. Anyhow after his death a subscription was raised to pay his debts. His end was a melancholy one, namely suicide, exactly like that of his uncle L.ᵈ Castlereagh, whom he resembled closely in manners and appearance. His character was in several respects one of the most noble which I have ever known, though tarnished by grave blemishes.

The voyage of the Beagle has been by far the most important event in my life and has determined my whole career; yet it depended on so small a circumstance as my Uncle offering to drive me 30 miles to Shrewsbury, which few uncles would have done, and on such a trifle as the shape of my nose. I have always felt that I owe to the Voyage the first real training or education of my mind. I was led to attend closely to several branches of natural history, and thus my powers of observation were improved, though they were already fairly developed. The investigation of the geology of all the places visited was far more important, as reasoning here comes into play. On first examining a new district nothing can appear more hopeless than the chaos of rocks; but by recording the stratification and nature of the rocks and fossils at many points, always reasoning and predicting what will be found elsewhere, light soon begins to dawn on the district, and the structure of the whole becomes more or less intelligible. I had brought with me the first volume of Lyell's Principles of Geology,[1] which I studied attentively; and this book was of the highest service to me in many ways. The very first place which I examined, namely St. Jago in the Cape Verde islands, showed me clearly the wonderful superiority of Lyell's manner of treating geology, compared with that of any other author, whose works I had with me or ever afterwards read. Another of my occupations was collecting animals of all classes, briefly describing and roughly dissecting many of the marine ones; but from not being able to draw and from not having sufficient anatomical knowledge a great pile of M.S which I made during the voyage has proved almost useless. I thus lost much time, with the exception of that spent in acquiring some knowledge of the Crustaceans, as this was of service when in after years I undertook a monograph of the Cirripedia. During some part of the day I wrote my Journal, and took much pains in describing carefully and vividly all that I had seen; and this was good practice. My Journal served, also, in part as letters to my home, and portions were sent to England, whenever there was an opportunity. The above various special studies were, however, of no importance compared with the habit of energetic industry and of concentrated attention to whatever I was engaged in, which I then acquired. Everything about which I thought or read was made to bear directly on what I had seen and was likely to see; and this habit of mind was continued during the five years of the voyage. I feel sure that it was this training which has enabled me to do whatever I have done in science.

Looking backwards, I can now perceive how my love for science gradually preponderated over every other taste. During the first two years my old passion for shooting survived in nearly full force, and I shot myself all the birds and animals for my collection; but gradually I gave up my gun more and more, and finally altogether to my servant, as shooting interfered with my work, more especially with making out the geological structure of a country. I discovered, though unconsciously and insensibly, that the pleasure of observing and reasoning was a much higher one that that of skill and sport. The primeval instincts of the barbarian slowly yielded to the acquired tastes of the civilized man. That my mind became developed through my pursuits during the voyage, is rendered probable by a remark made by my Father, who was the most acute observer whom I ever saw, of a sceptical disposition, and far from being a believer in phrenology; for on first seeing me after the Voyage, he turned round to my sisters, and exclaimed, 'Why, the shape of his head is quite altered.'

To return to the voyage. On September 11th (1831) I paid a flying visit with Fitz Roy to the Beagle at Plymouth. Thence to Shrewsbury to wish my Father and sisters a long farewell. On Oct. 24th, I took up my residence at Plymouth and remained there, until December 27th, when the Beagle finally left the shores of England for her circumnavigation of the world. We made two earlier attempts to sail, but were driven back each time by heavy gales. These two months at Plymouth were the most miserable which I ever spent, though I exerted myself in various ways. I was out of spirits at the thought of leaving all my family and friends for so long a time, and the weather seemed to me inexpressibly gloomy. I was also troubled with palpitations and pain about the heart, and like many a young ignorant man, especially one with a smattering of medical knowledge, was convinced that I had heart-disease. I did not consult any doctor, as I fully expected to hear the verdict that I was not fit for the voyage, and I was resolved to go at all hazards.

I need not here refer to the events of the Voyage,—where we went and what we did—as I have given a sufficiently full account in my published Journal. The glories of the vegetation of the Tropics rise before my mind at the present time more vividly than anything else. Though the sense of sublimity, which the great deserts of Patagonia and the forest-clad mountains of Tierra del Fuego excited in me, has left an indelible impression on my mind. The sight of a naked savage in his native land is an event which can never be forgotten. Many of my excursions on horseback through wild countries, or in the boats, some of which lasted several weeks, were deeply interesting; their discomfort and some degree of danger were at the time hardly a drawback and none at all afterwards. I also reflect with high satisfaction on some of my scientific work, such as solving the problem of coral-islands and making out the geological structure of certain islands, for instance St. Helena. Nor must I pass over the discovery of the singular relations of the animals and plants inhabiting the several islands of the Galapagos archipelago, and of all of them to the inhabitants of South America.

As far as I can judge of myself, I worked to the utmost during the voyage from the mere pleasure of investigation, and from my strong desire to add a few facts to the great mass of facts in natural science. But I was also ambitious to take a fair place amongst scientific men,— whether more ambitious or less so than most of my fellow-workers I can form no opinion.

The geology of St. Jago is very striking yet simple: a stream of lava formerly flowed over the bed of the sea, formed of triturated recent shells and corals, which it has baked into a hard white rock. Since then the whole island has been upheaved. But the line of white rock revealed to me a new and important fact, namely that there had been afterwards subsidence round the craters which had since been in action and had poured forth lava. It then first dawned on me that I might perhaps write a book on the geology of the various countries visited, and this made me thrill with delight. That was a memorable hour to me, and how distinctly I can call to mind the low cliff of lava beneath which I rested, with the sun glaring hot, a few strange desert plants growing near, and with living corals in the tidal pools at my feet. Later in the voyage Fitz Roy asked to read some of my Journal, and declared it would be worth publishing; so here was a second book in prospect!

Towards the close of our voyage I received a letter whilst at Ascension, in which my sisters told me that Sedgwick had called on my Father and said that I should take a place amongst the leading scientific men. I could not at the time understand how he could have learnt anything of my proceedings, but I heard (I believe afterwards) that Henslow had read some of the letters which I wrote to him before the Philosophical Soc. of Cambridge[1] and had printed them for private distribution. My collection of fossil bones, which had been sent to Henslow, also excited considerable attention amongst palaeontologists. After reading this letter I clambered over the mountains of Ascension with a bounding step, and made the volcanic rocks resound under my geological hammer! All this shows how ambitious I was; but I think that I can say with truth that in after years, though I cared in the highest degree for the approbation of such men as Lyell and Hooker, who were my friends, I did not care much about the general public. I do not mean to say that a favourable review or a large sale of my books did not please me greatly; but the pleasure was a fleeting one, and I am sure that I have never turned one inch out of my course to gain fame.

From my return to England (Oct. 2 1836) to my marriage (Jan. 29 1839)

THESE two years and three months were the most active ones which I ever spent, though I was occasionally unwell and so lost some time.

After going backwards and forwards several times between Shrewsbury, Maer, Cambridge and London, I settled in lodgings at Cambridge on December 13th, where all my collections were under the care of Henslow. I staid here three months and got my minerals and rocks examined by the aid of Prof. Miller. I began preparing my Journal of Travels, which was not hard work, as my M.S Journal had been written with care, and my chief labour was making an abstract of my more interesting scientific results. I sent also, at the request of Lyell, a short account of my observations on the elevation of the coast of Chile to the Geological Society. On March 7th 1837 I took lodgings in Great Marlborough St. in London and remained there for nearly two years until I was married. During these two years I finished my Journal, read several papers before the Geological Society, began preparing the MS for my Geological Observations and arranged for the publication of the Zoology of the Voyage of the Beagle. In July I opened my first note-book for facts in relation to the Origin of Species, about which I had long reflected, and never ceased working on for the next 20 years. During these two years I also went a little into society, and acted as one of the Hon. Secretaries of the Geological Society. I saw a great deal of Lyell. One of his chief characteristics was his sympathy with the work of others; and I was as much astonished as delighted at the interest which he showed when on my return to England I explained to him my views on coral-reefs. This encouraged me greatly, and his advice and example had much influence on me. During this time I saw also a good deal of Robert Brown 'facile princeps botanicorum.' I used often to call and sit with him during his breakfast on Sunday mornings, and he poured forth a rich treasure of curious observations and acute remarks, but they almost always related to minute points, and he never with me discussed large and general questions in science.

During these two years I took several short excursions as a relaxation, and one longer one to the parallel roads of Glen Roy, an account of which was published in the Philosophical Transactions. This paper was a great failure, and I am ashamed of it. Having been deeply impressed with what I had seen of the elevation of the land in S.

America, I attributed the parallel lines to the action of the sea; but I had to give up this view when Agassiz propounded his glacier-lake theory. Because no other explanation was possible under our then state of knowledge, I argued in favour of sea-action; and my error has been a good lesson to me never to trust in science to the principle of exclusion.

As I was not able to work all day at science I read a good deal during these two years on various subjects, including some metaphysical books, but I was not at [all] well fitted for such studies. About this time I took much delight in Wordsworth's and Coleridge's poetry, and can boast that I read the Excursion twice through. Formerly Milton's Paradise Lost had been my chief favourite, and in my excursions during the Voyage of the Beagle, when I could take only a single small volume, I always chose Milton.

Religious Belief

DURING these two years I was led to think much about religion. Whilst on board the Beagle I was quite orthodox, and I remember being heartily laughed at by several of the officers (though themselves orthodox) for quoting the Bible as an unanswerable authority on some point of morality. I suppose it was the novelty of the argument that amused them. But I had gradually come by this time (i.e. 1836 to 1839) to see that the Old Testament, from its manifestly false history of the world, with the Tower of Babel, the rain-bow as a sign, &c., &c., and from its attributing to God the feelings of a revengeful tyrant, was no more to be trusted than the sacred books of the Hindoos, or the beliefs of any barbarian. The question then continually rose before my mind and would not be banished,—is it credible that if God were now to make a revelation to the Hindoos, would he permit it to be connected with the belief in Vishnu, Siva, &c., as Christianity is connected with the Old Testament. This appeared to me utterly incredible. By further reflecting that the clearest evidence would be requisite to make any sane man believe in the miracles by which Christianity is supported,—that the more we know of the fixed laws of nature the more incredible do miracles become,—that the men at that time were ignorant and credulous to a degree almost incomprehensible by us—that the Gospels cannot be proved to have been written simultaneously with the events,—that they differ in many important details, far too important as it seemed to me to be admitted as the usual inaccuracies of eye-witnesses;—by such reflections as these which I give not as having the least novelty or value, but as they influenced me, I gradually came to disbelieve in Christianity as a divine revelation.

The fact that many false religions have spread over large portions of the earth like wild-fire had some weight with me. Beautiful as is the morality of the New Testament, it can hardly be denied that its perfection depends in part on the interpretation which we now put on metaphors and allegories. But I was very unwilling to give up my belief.—I feel sure of this for I can well remember often and often inventing day-dreams of old letters between distinguished Romans and manuscripts being discovered at Pompeii or elsewhere which confirmed in the most striking manner all that was written in the Gospels. But I found it more and more difficult, with free scope given to my imagination, to invent evidence which would suffice to convince me. Thus disbelief crept over me at a very slow rate, but was at last complete. The rate was so slow that I felt no distress, and have never since doubted even for a single second that my conclusion was correct. I can indeed hardly see how anyone ought to wish Christianity to be true; for if so, the plain language of the text seems to show that the men who do not believe, and this would include my Father, Brother and almost all my best friends, will be everlastingly punished.

And this is a damnable doctrine.

Although I did not think much about the existence of a personal God until a considerably later period of my life, I will here give the vague conclusions to which I have been driven. The old argument from design in nature, as given by Paley, which formerly seemed to me so conclusive, fails, now that the law of natural selection has been discovered. We can no longer argue that, for instance, the beautiful hinge of a bivalve shell must have been made by an intelligent being, like the hinge of a door by man. There seems to be no more design in the variability of organic beings and in the action of natural selection, than in the course which the wind blows. Everything in nature is the result of fixed laws. But I have discussed this subject at the end of my book on the Variation of Domesticated Animals and Plants, and the argument there given has never, as far as I can see, been answered.

But passing over the endless beautiful adaptations which we everywhere meet with, it may be asked how can the generally beneficent arrangement of the world be accounted for? Some writers indeed are so much impressed with the amount of suffering in the world, that they doubt if we look to all sentient beings, whether there is more of misery or of happiness,—whether the world as a whole is a good or bad one. According to my judgment happiness decidedly prevails, though this would be very difficult to prove. If the truth of this conclusion be granted it harmonises well with the effects which we might expect from natural selection. If all the individuals of any species were habitually to suffer to an extreme degree they would neglect to propagate their kind; but we have no reason to believe that this has ever or at least often occurred. Some other considerations, moreover, lead to the belief that all sentient beings have been formed so as to enjoy as a general rule happiness.

Every one who believes, as I do, that all the corporeal and mental organs (excepting those which are neither advantageous or disadvantageous to the possessor) of all beings have been developed through natural selection or the survival of the fittest, together with use or habit, will admit that these organs have been formed so that their possessors may compete successfully with other beings, and thus increase in number. Now an animal may be led to pursue that course of action which is the most beneficial to the species by suffering, such as pain, hunger, thirst and fear,—or by pleasure, as in eating and drinking and in the propagation of the species &c., or by both means combined as in the search for food. But pain or suffering of any kind, if long continued, causes depression and lessens the power of action; yet is well adapted to make a creature guard itself against any great or sudden evil. Pleasurable sensations, on the other hand may be long continued without any depressing effect; on the contrary they stimulate the whole system to increased action. Hence it has come to pass that most or all sentient beings have been developed in such a manner through natural selection that pleasurable sensations serve as their habitual guides. We see this in the pleasure from exertion, even occasionally from great exertion of the body or mind,—in the pleasure of our daily meals, and especially in the pleasure derived from sociability and from loving our families. The sum of such pleasures as these, which are habitual or frequently recurrent, give, as I can hardly doubt, to most sentient beings an excess of happiness over misery, although many occasionally suffer much. Such suffering, is quite compatible with the belief in natural selection, which is not perfect in its action, but tends only to render each species as successful as possible in the battle for life with other species under wonderfully complex and changing circumstances.

That there is much suffering in the world no one disputes. Some have attempted to explain this in reference to man; by imagining that it serves for his moral improvement. But the number of men in the world is as nothing compared with that of all other sentient beings, and these often suffer greatly without any moral improvement. A being so powerful and so full of knowledge as a God who could create the universe, is to our finite minds omnipotent and omniscient, and it revolts our understanding to suppose that his benevolence is not unbounded, for what advantage can there be in the sufferings of millions of the lower animals throughout almost endless time? This very old argument from the existence of suffering against the existence of an intelligent first cause seems to me a strong one; whereas, as just remarked, the presence of much suffering agrees well with the view that all organic beings have been developed through variation and natural selection.

At the present day the most usual argument for the existence of an intelligent God is drawn from deep inward conviction and feelings which are experienced by most persons. But it cannot be doubted that Hindoos, Mahomedans and others might argue in the same manner and with equal force in favour of the existence of one God, or of many Gods, or as with the Buddists of no God. There are also many barbarian tribes who cannot be said with any truth to believe in what we call God: they believe indeed in spirits or ghosts, and it can be explained, as Tyler and Herbert Spencer have shown, how such a belief would be likely to arise.

Formerly I was led by feelings such as those just referred to, (although I do not think that the religious sentiment was ever strongly developed in me) to the firm conviction of the existence of God, and of the immortality of the soul. In my Journal I wrote that whilst standing in the midst of the grandeur of a Brazilian forest, 'it is not possible to give an adequate idea of the higher feelings of wonder, admiration and devotion, which fill and elevate the mind.' I well remember my conviction that there is more in man than the mere breath of his body. But now the grandest scenes would not cause any such convictions and feelings to rise in my mind. It may be truly said that I am like a man who has become colour-blind, and the universal belief by men of the existence of redness makes my present loss of perception of not the least value as evidence. This argument would be a valid one, if all men of all races had the same inward conviction of the existence of one God; but we know that this is very far from being the case. Therefore I cannot see that such inward convictions and feelings are of any weight as evidence of what really exists. The state of mind which grand scenes formerly excited in me, and which was intimately connected with a belief in God, did not essentially differ from that which is often called the sense of sublimity; and however difficult it may be to explain the genesis of this sense, it can hardly be advanced as an argument for the existence of God, any more than the powerful though vague and similar feelings excited by music.

With respect to immortality, nothing shows me how strong and almost instinctive a belief it is, as the consideration of the view now held by most physicists, namely that the sun with all the planets will in time grow too cold for life, unless indeed some great body dashes into the sun and thus gives it fresh life.—Believing as I do that man in the distant future will be a far more perfect creature than he now is, it is an intolerable thought that he and all other sentient beings are doomed to complete annihilation after such long-continued slow progress. To those who fully admit the immortality of the human soul, the destruction of our world will not appear so dreadful.

Another source of conviction in the existence of God, connected with the reason and not with the feelings, impresses me as having much more weight. This follows from the extreme difficulty or rather impossibility of conceiving this immense and wonderful universe, including man with his capacity of looking far backward and far into futurity, as the result of blind chance or necessity. When thus reflecting I feel compelled to look to a First Cause having an intelligent mind in some degree analogous to that of man; and I deserve to be called a Theist.

This conclusion was strong in my mind about the time, as far as I can remember, when I wrote the Origin of Species; and it is since that time that it has very gradually with many fluctuations become weaker.[1] But then arises the doubt—can the mind of man, which has, as I fully believe, been developed from a mind as low as that possessed by the lowest animal, be trusted when it draws such grand conclusions? May not these be the result of the connection between cause and effect which strikes us as a necessary one, but probably depends merely on inherited experience? Nor must we overlook the probability of the constant inculcation of a belief in God on the minds of children producing so strong and perhaps an inherited effect on their brains, not as yet fully developed, that it would be as difficult for them to throw off their belief in God, as for a monkey to throw off its instinctive fear and hatred of a snake. I cannot pretend to throw the least light on such abstruse problems. The mystery of the beginning of all things is insoluble by us; and I for one must be content to remain an Agnostic.

A man who has no assured and ever present belief in the existence of a personal God or of a future existence with retribution and reward, can have for his rule of life, as far as I can see, only to follow those impulses and instincts which are the strongest or which seem to

Sir Joseph Dalton Hooker,
c. 1850

Alfred Russel Wallace,
c. 1860

Sir Richard Owen

him the best ones. A dog acts in this manner, but he does so blindly. A man, on the other hand, looks forward and backwards, and compares his various feelings, desires and recollections. He then finds, in accordance with the verdict of all the wisest men, that the highest satisfaction is derived from following certain impulses, namely the social instincts. If he acts for the good of others, he will receive the approbation of his fellow-men and gain the love of those with whom he lives; and this latter gain undoubtedly is the highest pleasure on this earth. By degrees it will become intolerable to him to obey his sensuous passions rather than his higher impulses, which when rendered habitual may be almost called instincts. His reason may occasionally tell him to act in opposition to the opinion of others, whose approbation he will then not receive; but he will still have the solid satisfaction of knowing that he has followed his innermost guide or conscience.—As for myself I believe that I have acted rightly in steadily following and devoting my life to science. I feel no remorse from having committed any great sin, but have often and often regretted that I have not done more direct good to my fellow-creatures. My sole and poor excuse is much ill-health, and my mental constitution which makes it extremely difficult for me to turn from one subject or occupation to another. I can imagine with high satisfaction giving up my whole time to philanthropy, but not a portion of it; though this would have been a far better line of conduct.

Nothing is more remarkable than the spread of scepticism or rationalism during the latter half of my life. Before I was engaged to be married, my father advised me to conceal carefully my doubts, for he said that he had known extreme misery thus caused with married persons. Things went on pretty well until the wife or husband became out of health, and then some women suffered miserably by doubting about the salvation of their husbands, thus making them likewise to suffer. My father added that he had known during his whole long life only three women who were sceptics; and it should be remembered that he knew well a multitude of persons and possessed extraordinary powers of winning confidence. When I asked him who the three women were, he had to own with respect to one of them, his sister-in-law, Kitty Wedgwood, that he had no good evidence, only the vaguest hints, aided by the conviction that so clear-sighted a woman could not be a believer. At the present time, with my small acquaintance I know (or have known) several married ladies, who believe very little more than their husbands. My father used to quote an unanswerable argument, by which an old lady, a Mrs. Barlow, who suspected him of unorthodoxy, hoped to convert him: 'Doctor, I know that sugar is sweet in my mouth, and I know that my Redeemer liveth.'

From my marriage, Jan. 29th 1839, and residence in
Upper Gower St. to our leaving London and settling at
Down, Sep. 14th 1842

YOU all know well your Mother,[1] and what a good Mother she has ever been to all of you. She has been my greatest blessing, and I can declare that in my whole life I have never heard her utter one word which I would rather have been unsaid. She has never failed in the kindest sympathy towards me, and has borne with the utmost patience my frequent complaints from ill-health and discomfort. I do not believe she has ever missed an opportunity of doing a kind action to anyone near her. I marvel at my good fortune that she, so infinitely my superior in every single moral quality, consented to be my wife. She has been my wise adviser and cheerful comforter throughout life, which without her would have been during a very long period a miserable one from ill-health. She has earned the love and admiration of every soul near her.

(Mem: her beautiful letter to myself preserved, shortly after our marriage.)

I have indeed been most happy in my family, and I must say to you my children that not one of you has ever given me one minutes anxiety, except on the score of health. There are, I suspect very few fathers of five sons who could say this with entire truth. When you were very young it was my delight to play with you all, and I think with a sigh that such days can never return. From your earliest days to now that you are grown up, you have all, sons and daughters, ever been most pleasant, sympathetic and affectionate to us and to one another. When all or most of you are at home (as thank Heavens happens pretty frequently) no party can be, according to my taste, more agreeable, and I wish for no other society. We have suffered only one very severe grief in the death of Annie at Malvern on April 24th 1851, when she was just over ten years old. She was a most sweet and affectionate child, and I feel sure would have grown into a delightful woman. But I need say nothing here of her character, as I wrote a short sketch of it shortly after her death. Tears still sometimes come into my eyes, when I think of her sweet ways.

During the three years and eight months whilst we resided in London,[1] I did less scientific work, though I worked as hard as I possibly could, than during any other equal length of time in my life. This was owing to frequently recurrent unwellness and to one long and serious illness. The greater part of my time, when I could do anything, was devoted to my work on Coral Reefs, which I had begun before my marriage, and of which the last proof-sheet was corrected on May 6th 1842. This book, though a small one, cost me 20 months of hard work, as I had to read every work on the islands of the Pacific and to consult many charts. It was thought highly of by scientific men, and the theory therein given, is, I think now well established.

No other work of mine was begun in so deductive a spirit as this; for the whole theory was thought out on the west coast of S. America before I had seen a true coral-reef. I had therefore only to verify and extend my views by a careful examination of living reefs. But it should be observed that I had during the two previous years been incessantly attending to the effects on the shores of S. America of the intermittent elevation of the land, together with denudation and the deposition of sediment. This necessarily led me to reflect much on the effects of subsidence, and it was easy to replace in imagination the continued deposition of sediment by the upward growth of coral. To do this was to form my theory of the formation of barrier-reefs and atolls.

Besides my work on coral-reefs, during my residence in London, I read before the Geological Society papers[1] on the Erratic Boulders of S. America, on Earthquakes, and on the formation by the agency of earth-worms of mould. I also continued to superintend the publication of the Zoology of the Voyage of the Beagle.[2] Nor did I ever intermit collecting facts bearing on the origin of species; and I could sometimes do this when I could do nothing else from illness. In the summer of 1842 I was stronger than I had been for some time and took a little tour by myself in N. Wales, for the sake of observing the effects of the old glaciers which formerly filled all the larger valleys. I published a short account of what I saw in the Philosophical Magazine.[3] This excursion interested me greatly, and it was the last time I was ever strong enough to climb mountains or to take long walks, such as are necessary for geological work.

During the early part of our life in London, I was strong enough to go into general society and saw a good deal of several scientific men, and other more or less distinguished men. I will give my impressions with respect to some of them, though I have little to say worth saying.

I saw more of Lyell than of any other man both before and after my marriage. His mind was characterised, as it appeared to me, by clearness, caution, sound judgment and a good deal of originality. When I made any remark to him on geology, he never rested until he saw the whole case clearly, and often made me see it more clearly than I had done before. He would advance all possible objections to my suggestion, and even after these were exhausted would long remain dubious. A second characteristic was his hearty sympathy with the work of other scientific men. On my return from the voyage of the Beagle, I explained to him my views on coral-reefs, which differed from his, and I was greatly surprised and encouraged by the vivid interest which he showed. On such occasions, while absorbed in thought, he would throw himself into the strangest attitudes, often resting his head on the seat of a chair, while standing up. His delight in science was ardent, and he felt the keenest interest in the future progress of mankind. He was very kind-hearted, and thoroughly liberal in his religious beliefs or rather disbeliefs; but he was a strong theist. His candour was highly remarkable. He exhibited this by becoming a convert to the Descent-theory, though he had gained much fame by opposing Lamarck's views, and this after he had grown old. He reminded me that I had many years before said to him, when discussing the opposition of the old school of geologists to his new views, 'What a good thing it would be, if every scientific man was to die when 60 years old, as afterwards he would be sure to oppose all new doctrines.' But he hoped that now he might be allowed to live. He had a strong sense of humour and often told amusing anecdotes. He was very fond of society, especially of eminent men and of persons high in rank; and this over-estimation of a man's position in the world, seemed to me his chief foible. He used to discuss with Lady Lyell as a most serious question, whether or not they should accept some particular invitation. But as he would not dine out more than three times a week on account of the loss of time, he was justified in weighing his invitations with some care. He looked forward to going out oftener in the evening with advancing years, as to a great reward; but the good time never came, as his strength failed.

The science of geology is enormously indebted to Lyell, more so, as I believe, than to any other man who ever lived. When [I was] starting on the voyage of the Beagle, the sagacious Henslow, who like all other geologists believed at that time in successive cataclysms, advised me to get and study the first volume of the Principles, which had then just been published, but on no account to accept the views therein advocated. How differently would any one now speak of the Principles! I am proud to remember that the first place, namely St. Jago, in the Cape Verde Archipelago, which I geologised, convinced me of the infinite superiority of Lyell's views over those advocated in any other work known to me. The powerful effects of Lyells works could formerly be plainly seen in the different progress of the science in France and England. The present total oblivion of Elie de Beaumonts wild hypotheses, such as his 'Craters of Elevation' and 'Lines of Elevation' (which latter hypothesis I heard Sedgwick at the

Geolog. Soc. lauding to the skies), may be largely attributed to Lyell.

All the leading geologists were more or less known by me at the time when geology was advancing with triumphant steps. I liked most of them, with the exception of Buckland, who though very good-humoured and good-natured seemed to me a vulgar and almost coarse man. He was incited more by a craving for notoriety, which sometimes made him act like a buffoon, than by a love of science. He was not, however, selfish in his desire for notoriety; for Lyell, when a very young man, consulted him about communicating a poor paper to the Geolog. Soc. which had been sent him by a stranger, and Buckland answered 'You had better do so, for it will be headed, "Communicated by Charles Lyell", and thus your name will be brought before the public.'

The services rendered to geology by Murchison by his classification of the older formations cannot be over-estimated; but he was very far from possessing a philosophical mind. He was very kind-hearted and would exert himself to the utmost to oblige anyone. The degree to which he valued rank was ludicrous, and he displayed this feeling and his vanity with the simplicity of a child. He related with the utmost glee to a large circle, including many mere acquaintances, in the rooms of the Geolog. Soc. how the Czar Nicholas, when in London, had patted him on the shoulder and had said, alluding to his geological work, 'Mon ami, Russia is grateful to you'; and then Murchison added, rubbing his hands together, 'The best of it was that Prince Albert heard it all.' He announced one day to the Council of the Geolog. Soc. that his great work on the Silurian system was at last published; and he then looked at all who were present and said, 'You will every one of you find your name in the Index,' as if this was the height of glory.

I saw a good deal of R. Brown, 'facile Princeps Botanicorum,' as he was called by Humboldt; and before I was married I used to go and sit with him almost every Sunday morning. He seemed to me to be chiefly remarkable for the minuteness of his observations and their perfect accuracy. He never propounded to me any large scientific views in biology. His knowledge was extraordinarily great, and much died with him, owing to his excessive fear of ever making a mistake. He poured out his knowledge to me in the most unreserved manner, yet was strangely jealous on some points. I called on him two or three times before the voyage of the Beagle, and on one occasion he asked me to look through a microscope and describe what I saw. This I did, and believe now that it was the marvellous currents of protoplasm in some vegetable cell. I then asked him what I had seen; but he answered me, who was then hardly more than a boy and on the point of leaving England for five years, 'That is my little secret.' I suppose that he was afraid that I might steal his discovery. Hooker told me that he was a complete miser, and knew himself to be a miser, about his dried plants; and he would not lend specimens to Hooker, who was describing the plants of Tierra del Fuego, although well knowing that he himself would never make any use of the collections from this country. On the other hand he was capable of the most generous actions. When old, much out of health and quite unfit for any exertion, he daily visited (as Hooker told me) an old man-servant, who lived at a distance and whom he supported, and read aloud to him. This is enough to make up for any degree of scientific penuriousness or jealousy. He was rather given to sneering at anyone who wrote about what he did not fully understand: I remember praising Whewell's History of the Inductive Sciences to him, and he answered, 'Yes, I suppose that he has read the prefaces of very many books.'

I often saw Owen, whilst living in London, and admired him greatly, but was never able to understand his character and never became intimate with him. After the publication of the Origin of Species he became my bitter enemy, not owing to any quarrel between us, but as far as I could judge out of jealousy at its success. Poor dear Falconer, who was a charming man, had a very bad opinion of him, being convinced that he was not only ambitious, very envious and arrogant, but untruthful and dishonest. His power of hatred was certainly unsurpassed. When in former days I used to defend Owen, Falconer often said 'You will find him out[1] some day,' and so it has proved.

At a somewhat later period I became very intimate with Hooker, who has been one of my best friends throughout life. He is a delightfully pleasant companion and most kind-hearted. One can see at once that he is honourable to the back-bone. His intellect is very acute, and he has great power of generalisation. He is the most untirable worker that I have ever seen, and will sit the whole day working with the microscope, and be in the evening as fresh and pleasant as ever. He is in all ways very impulsive and somewhat peppery in temper; but the clouds pass away almost immediately. He once sent me an almost savage letter from a cause which will appear ludicrously small to an outsider, viz. because I maintained for a time the silly notion that our coal-plants had lived in shallow water in the sea. His indignation was all the greater because he could not pretend that he should ever have suspected that the Mangrove (and a few other marine plants which I named) had lived in the sea, if they had been found only in a fossil state. On another occasion he was almost equally indignant because I rejected with scorn the notion that a continent had formerly extended between Australia and S. America. I have known hardly any man more loveable than Hooker.

A little later I became intimate with Huxley. His mind is as quick as a flash of lightning and as sharp as a razor. He is the best talker whom I have known. He never says and never writes anything flat. From his conversation no one would suppose that he could cut up his opponents in so trenchant a manner as he can do and does do. He has been a most kind friend to me and would always take any trouble for me. He has been the mainstay in England of the principle of the gradual evolution of organic beings. Much splendid work as he has done in Zoology, he would have done far more, if his time had not been so largely consumed by official and literary work, and by his efforts to improve the education of the country. He would allow me to say anything to him: many years ago I thought that it was a pity that he attacked so many scientific men, although I believe that he was right in each particular case, and I said so to him. He denied the charge indignantly, and I answered that I was very glad to hear that I was mistaken. We had been talking about his well-deserved attacks on Owen, so I said after a time, 'How well you have exposed Ehrenberg's[1] blunders;' he agreed and added that it was necessary for science that such mistakes should be exposed. Again after a time, I added, 'Poor Agassiz[2] has fared ill under your hands.' Again I added another name, and now his bright eyes flashed on me, and he burst out laughing, anathematising me in some manner. He is a splendid man and has worked well for the good of mankind.

I may here mention a few other eminent men, whom I have occasionally seen, but I have little to say about them worth saying. I felt a high reverence for Sir J. Herschel, and was delighted to dine with him at his charming house at the C. of Good Hope, and afterwards at his London house. I saw him, also, on a few other occasions. He never talked much, but every word which he uttered was worth listening to. He was very shy and he often had a distressed expression. Lady Caroline Bell, at whose house I dined at the C. of Good Hope, admired Herschel much, but said that he always came into a room, as if he knew that his hands were dirty, and that he knew that his wife knew that they were dirty.

I once met at breakfast at Sir R. Murchison's house the illustrious Humboldt, who honoured me by expressing a wish to see me. I was a little disappointed with the great man, but my anticipations probably were too high. I can remember nothing distinctly about our interview, except that Humboldt was very cheerful and talked much.

I used to call pretty often on Babbage and regularly attended his famous evening parties. He was always worth listening to, but he was a disappointed and discontented man; and his expression was often or generally morose. I do not believe that he was half as sullen as he pretended to be. One day he told me that he had invented a plan by which all fires could be effectually stopped, but added, 'I shan't publish it—damn them all, let all their houses be burnt.' The all were the inhabitants of London. Another day he told me that he had seen a pump on a road-side in Italy, with a pious inscription on it to the effect that the owner had erected the pump for the love of God and his country, that the tired way-farer might drink. This led Babbage to examine the pump closely and he soon discovered that every time that a way-farer pumped some water for himself, he pumped a larger quantity into the owner's house. Babbage then added 'There is only one thing which I hate more than piety, and that is patriotism.' But I believe that his bark was much worse than his bite.

Herbert Spencer's conversation seemed to me very interesting, but I did not like him particularly and did not feel that I could easily have become intimate with him. I think that he was extremely egotistical. After reading any of his books I generally feel enthusiastic admiration of his transcendent talents, and have often wondered whether in the distant future he would rank with such great men, as Descartes, Leibnitz &c., about whom, however, I know very little. Nevertheless I am not conscious of having profited in my own work by Spencer's writings. His deductive manner of treating every subject is wholly opposed to my frame of mind. His conclusions never convince me: and over and over again I have said to myself, after reading one of his discussions, 'Here would be a fine subject for half-a-dozen years work.' His fundamental generalisations, (which have been compared in importance by some persons with Newton's laws!) which I daresay may be very valuable under a philosophical point of view, are of such a nature that they do not seem to me to be of any strictly scientific use. They partake more of the nature of definitions than of laws of nature. They do not aid one in predicting what will happen in any particular case. Anyhow they have not been of any use to me.

Speaking of H. Spencer reminds me of Buckle, whom I once met at Hensleigh Wedgwood's. I was very glad to learn from him his system of collecting facts. He told me that he bought all the books which he read, and made a full index to each of the facts which he thought might prove serviceable to him, and that he could always remember in what book he had read anything, for his memory was wonderful. I then asked him how at first he could judge what facts would be serviceable, and he answered that he did not know, but that a sort of instinct guided him. From this habit of making indices he was enabled to give the astonishing number of references on all sorts of subjects, which may be found in his History of Civilisation.[1] This book I thought most interesting and read it twice; but I doubt whether his generalisations are worth anything. H. Spencer told me that he had never read a line of it! Buckle was a great talker, and I listened to him without saying hardly a word; nor indeed could I have done so, for he left no gaps. When Effie[2] began to sing, I jumped up and said that I must listen to her. This, I suppose, offended him, for after I had moved away, he turned round to a friend, and said (as was overheard by my brother), 'Well Mr. Darwin's books are much better than his conversation.' What he really meant, was that I did not properly appreciate his conversation.

Of other great literary men, I once met Sidney Smith at Dean Milman's house. There was something inexplicably amusing in every word which he uttered. Perhaps this was partly due to the expectation of being amused. He was talking about Lady Cork, who was then extremely old. This was the lady, who, as he said, was once so much affected by one of his charity sermons, that she *borrowed* a guinea from a friend to put into the Plate. He now said, 'It is generally believed that my dear old friend Lady Cork has been overlooked'; and he said this in such a manner that no one could for a moment doubt that he meant that his dear old friend had been overlooked by the Devil. How he managed to express this, I know not.

I likewise once met Macaulay at L.ᵈ Stanhope's (the historian's) house, and as there was only one other man at dinner, I had a grand opportunity of hearing him converse, and he was very agreeable. He did not talk at all too much; nor indeed could such a man talk too much as long as he allowed others to turn the stream of his conversation, and this he did allow. L.ᵈ Stanhope once gave me a curious little proof of the accuracy and fulness of Macaulay's memory: many historians used often to meet at L.ᵈ Stanhope's house, and in discussing various subjects they would sometimes differ from Macaulay, and formerly they often referred to some book to see who was right; but latterly, as L.ᵈ Stanhope noticed, no historian ever took this trouble, and whatever Macaulay said was final.

On another occasion I met at L.ᵈ Stanhope's house one of his parties of historians and other literary men, and amongst them were Motley and Grote. After luncheon I walked about Chevening Park for nearly an hour with Grote, and was much interested by his conversation and pleased by the simplicity and absence of all pretension in his manners. I met another set of great men at breakfast at L. Stanhope's house in London. After breakfast was quite over, Monckton Milnes (L. Houghton now) walked in, and after looking round, exclaimed (justifying Sidney Smith's nickname of 'the cool of the evening') 'Well I declare you are all very premature.'

Long ago I dined occasionally with the old Earl [Stanhope], the father of the historian. I have heard that his father, the democratic earl, well-known at the time of the French Revolution, had his son educated as a blacksmith, as he declared that every man ought to know some trade. The old Earl, whom I knew, was a strange man, but what little I saw of him, I liked much. He was frank, genial, and pleasant. He had strongly marked features, with a brown complexion, and his clothes, when I saw him, were all brown. He seemed to believe in everything which was to others utterly incredible. He said one day to me, 'Why don't you give up your fiddle-faddle of geology and zoology, and turn to the occult sciences?' The historian (then L. Mahon) seemed shocked at such a speech to me, and his charming wife much amused.

The last man whom I will mention is Carlyle,[1] seen by me several times at my brother's house and 2 or 3 times at my own house. His talk was very racy and interesting, just like his writings, but he sometimes went on too long on the same subject. I remember a funny dinner at my brother's, where amongst a few others were Babbage and Lyell, both of whom liked to talk. Carlyle, however, silenced everyone by haranguing during the whole dinner—on the advantages of silence. After dinner Babbage in his grimmest manner thanked Carlyle for his very interesting Lecture on Silence.

Carlyle sneered at almost everyone: one day in my house, he called Grote's History 'a fetid quagmire, with nothing spiritual about it.' I always thought until his Reminiscences appeared, that his sneers were partly jokes, but this now seems rather doubtful. His expression was that of a depressed, almost despondent, yet benevolent man; and it is notorious how heartily he laughed. I believe that his benevolence was real, though stained by not a little jealousy. No one can doubt about his extraordinary power of drawing vivid pictures of things and men,—far more vivid, as it appears to me, than any drawn by Macaulay. Whether his pictures of men were true ones is another question. He has been all powerful in impressing some grand moral truths on the minds of men. On the other hand his views about slavery were revolting. In his eyes might was right. His mind seemed to me a very narrow one; even if all branches of science, which he despised, are excluded. It is astonishing to me that Kingsley should have spoken of him, as a man well fitted to advance science. He laughed to scorn the idea that a mathematician, such as Whewell, could judge, as I maintained he could, of Goethe's views on light.[1] He thought it a most ridiculous thing that anyone should care whether a glacier moved a little quicker or a little slower, or moved at all. As far as I could judge, I never met a man with a mind so ill adapted for scientific research.

Whilst living in London, I attended as regularly as I could the meetings of several Scientific societies, and acted as Secretary to the Geological Soc? But such attendance and ordinary society suited my health so badly that we resolved to live in the country, which we both preferred and have never repented of.

Residence at Down from Sep. 14 1842 to the present time, 1876

AFTER several fruitless searches in Surrey and elsewhere, we found this house and purchased it. I was pleased with the diversified appearance of the vegetation, proper to a chalk district, and so unlike what I had been accustomed to in the midland counties; and still more pleased with the extreme quietness and rusticity of the place. It is not, however, quite so retired a place as a writer in a German periodical makes it, who says that my house can be approached only by a mule track! Our fixing ourselves here has answered admirably in one way, which we did not anticipate, namely by being very convenient for frequent visits from our children, who never miss an opportunity of doing so when they can.

Few persons can have lived a more retired life than we have done. Besides short visits to the houses of relations, and occasionally to the sea-side or elsewhere, we have gone nowhere. During the first part of our residence we went a little into society, and received a few friends here; but my health almost always suffered from the excitement, violent shivering and vomiting attacks being thus brought on. I have therefore been compelled for many years to give up all dinner-parties; and this has been somewhat of a deprivation to me, as such parties always put me into high spirits. From the same cause I have been able to invite here very few scientific acquaintances. Whilst I was young and strong I was capable of very warm attachments, but of late years, though I still have very friendly feelings towards many persons, I have lost the power of becoming deeply attached to anyone, not even so deeply to my good and dear friends Hooker and Huxley, as I should formerly have been. As far as I can judge this grievous loss of feeling has gradually crept over me, from the expectation of much distress afterwards, from exhaustion having become firmly associated in my mind with seeing and talking with anyone for an hour, except my wife and children.

My chief enjoyment and sole employment throughout life has been scientific work; and the excitement from such work makes me for the time forget or drives quite away my daily discomfort. I have therefore nothing to record during the rest of my life, except the publication of my several books. Perhaps a few details how they arose may be worth giving.

My Several Publications

IN the early part of 1844, my observations on the Volcanic Islands visited during the voyage of the Beagle were published. In 1845 I took much pains in correcting a new edition of my Journal of Researches, which was originally published in 1839 as part of Fitz Roy's work. The success of this my first literary child always tickles my vanity more than that of any of my other books. Even to this day it sells steadily in England and the United States, and has been translated for the second time into German, and into French and other languages. This success of a book of travels, especially of a scientific one, so many years after its first publication, is surprising. Ten thousand copies have now been sold in England of the second edition. In 1846 my geological observations on S. America were published. I record in a little diary which I have always kept, that my three geological books (Coral-Reefs included) consumed four and a half years steady work; 'and now it is ten years since my return to England. How much time have I lost by illness.' I have nothing to say about these three books, except that to my surprise new editions have lately been called for.

In October 1846 I began to work on Cirripedia.[1] When on the coast of Chile I found a most curious form, which burrowed into the shells of Concholepas, and which differed so much from all other cirripedes that I had to form a new sub-order for its sole reception. Lately an allied burrowing genus has been found on the shores of Portugal. To understand the structure of my new cirripede I had to examine and dissect many of the common forms; and this gradually led me on to take up the whole group. I worked steadily on the subject for the next eight years, and ultimately published two thick volumes describing all the known living species and two thin quartos on the extinct species. I do not doubt that Sir E. Lytton Bulwer had me in his mind, when he introduces in one of his novels, a Professor Long who had written two huge volumes on Limpets. Although I was employed during eight years on this work, yet I record in my diary that about two years out of this time was lost by illness. On this account I went in 1848 for some months to Malvern for hydropathic treatment, which did me much good so that on my return home I was able to resume work. So much was I out of health that when my dear Father died on November 13th 1847 I was unable to attend his funeral or to act as one of his executors.

My work on the Cirripedia possesses, I think, considerable value, as besides describing several new and remarkable forms, I made out the homologies of the various parts—I discovered the cementing apparatus, though I blundered dreadfully about the cement-glands —and lastly I proved the existence in certain genera of minute males complemental to and parasitic on the hermaphrodites. This latter discovery has at last been fully confirmed; though at one time a German writer was pleased to attribute the whole account to my fertile imagination. The cirripedes form a highly varying and difficult group of species to class; and my work was of considerable use to me, when I had to discuss in the Origin of Species the principles of a natural classification. Nevertheless I doubt whether the work was worth the consumption of so much time.

From September 1854 onwards I devoted all my time to arranging my huge pile of notes, to observing and experimenting, in relation to the transmutation of species. During the voyage of the Beagle I had been deeply impressed by discovering in the Pampean formation great fossil animals covered with armour like that on the existing armadillos; secondly by the manner in which closely allied animals replace one another in proceeding southwards over the Continent; and thirdly by the South American character of most of the productions of the Galapagos archipelago, and more especially by the manner in which they differ slightly on each island of the group; none of these islands appearing to be very ancient in a geological sense. It was evident that such facts as these as well as many others could be explained on the supposition that species gradually become modified; and the subject haunted me. But it was equally evident that neither the action of the surrounding conditions, nor the will of the organisms (especially in the case of plants), could account for the innumerable cases in which organisms of every kind are beautifully adapted to their habits of life,—for instance a woodpecker or tree-frog to climb trees, or a seed for dispersal by hooks or plumes. I had always been much struck by such adaptations, and until these could be explained it seemed to me almost useless to endeavour to prove by indirect evidence that species have been modified.

After my return to England it appeared to me that by following the example of Lyell in Geology, and by collecting all facts which

Charles Darwin, 1881

Down House, view from the garden, 1882

Charles Darwin's study at Down House at the same date

bore in any way on the variation of animals and plants under domestication and nature, some light might perhaps be thrown on the whole subject. My first note-book[1] was opened in July 1837. I worked on true Baconian principles, and without any theory collected facts on a whole-sale scale, more especially with respect to domesticated productions, by printed enquiries, by conversation with skilful breeders and gardeners, and by extensive reading. When I see the list of books of all kinds which I read and abstracted, including whole series of Journals and Transactions, I am surprised at my industry. I soon perceived that Selection was the key-stone of man's success in making useful races of animals and plants. But how selection could be applied to organisms living in a state of nature remained for some time a mystery to me. In October 1838, that is fifteen months after I had begun my systematic enquiry, I happened to read for amusement 'Malthus on Population', and being well prepared to appreciate the struggle for existence which everywhere goes on from long-continued observation of the habits of animals and plants, it at once struck me that under these circumstances favourable variations would tend to be preserved and unfavourable ones to be destroyed. The result of this would be the formation of new species.

Here then I had at last got a theory by which to work; but I was so anxious to avoid prejudice, that I determined not for some time to write even the briefest sketch of it. In June 1842 I first allowed myself the satisfaction of writing a very brief abstract of my theory in pencil in 35 pages; and this was enlarged during the summer of 1844 into one of 230 pages, which I had fairly copied out and still possess.[2] But at that time I overlooked one problem of great importance; and it is astonishing to me, except on the principle of Columbus and his egg, how I could have overlooked it and its solution. This problem is the tendency in organic beings descended from the same stock to diverge in character as they become modified. That they have diverged greatly is obvious from the manner in which species of all kinds can be classed under genera, genera under families, families under sub-orders, and so forth; and I can remember the very spot in the road whilst in my carriage, when to my joy the solution occurred to me; and this was long after I had come to Down. The solution, as I believe, is that the modified offspring of all dominant and increasing forms tend to become adapted to many and highly diversified places in the economy of nature.

Early in 1856 Lyell advised me to write out my views pretty fully, and I began at once to do so on a scale three or four times as extensive as that which was afterwards followed in my Origin of Species; yet it was only an abstract of the materials which I had collected, and I got through about half the work on this scale. But my plans were overthrown, for early in the summer of 1858 Mr. Wallace, who was then in the Malay Archipelago, sent me an essay 'On the tendency of varieties to depart indefinitely from the original type'; and this essay contained exactly the same theory as mine. Mr. Wallace expressed the wish that if I thought well of his essay, I should send it to Lyell for perusal. The circumstances under which I consented at the request of Lyell and Hooker to allow of an extract from my M.S, together with a letter to Asa Gray dated September 5 1857, to be published at the same time with Wallace's Essay, are given in the Journal of the Proceedings of the Linn. Soc. 1858 p. 45. I was at first very unwilling to consent, as I thought Mr. Wallace might consider my doing so unjustifiable, for I did not then know how generous and noble was his disposition. The extract from my M.S and the letter to Asa Gray had neither been intended for publication and were badly written. Mr. Wallace's essay, on the other hand was admirably expressed and quite clear. Nevertheless our joint productions excited very little attention, and the only published notice of them which I can remember was by Prof. Haughton of Dublin, whose verdict was that all that was new in them was false, and what was true was old. This shows how necessary it is that any new view should be explained at considerable length in order to arouse public attention.

In September 1858 I set to work by the strong advice of Lyell and Hooker to prepare a volume on the transmutation of species, but was often interrupted by ill-health, and short visits to Dr. Lane's delightful hydropathic establishment at Moor Park. I abstracted the M.S begun on a much larger scale in 1856, and completed the volume on the same reduced scale. It cost me 13 months and ten days hard labour. It was published under the title of the 'Origin of Species'[1] in November 1859. Though considerably added to and corrected in the later editions it has remained substantially the same book.

It is no doubt the chief work of my life. It was from the first highly successful. The first small edition of 1250 copies was sold on the day of publication, and a second edition of 3000 copies soon afterwards. Sixteen thousand copies have now (1876) been sold in England, and considering how stiff a book it is this is a large sale. It has been translated into almost every European tongue, even into such languages as Spanish, Bohemian, Polish and Russian. It has also, according to Miss Bird, been translated into Japanese, and is there much studied. Even an essay in Hebrew has appeared on it, showing that the theory is contained in the Old Testament! The Reviews were very numerous; for a time I collected all that appeared on the Origin and on my related books, and these amount (excluding newspaper reviews) to 265; but after a time I gave up the attempt in despair. Many separate essays and books on the subject have appeared; and in Germany a catalogue or Bibliography on 'Darwinismus' has appeared every year or two.

The success of the Origin may, I think, be attributed in large part to my having long before written two condensed sketches, and to my having finally abstracted a much larger manuscript, which was itself an abstract. By this means I was enabled to select the more striking facts and conclusions. I had, also, during many years, followed a golden rule, namely that whenever a published fact, a new observation or thought came across me, which was opposed to my general results, to make a memorandum of it without fail and at once; for I had found by experience that such facts and thoughts were far more apt to escape from the memory, than favourable ones. Owing to this habit, very few objections were raised against my views which I had not at least noticed and attempted to answer. It has sometimes been said that the success of the Origin proved 'that the subject was in the air' or 'that men's minds were prepared for it.' I do not think that this is strictly true, for I occasionally sounded not a few naturalists, and never happened to come across a single one who seemed to doubt about the permanence of species. Even Lyell and Hooker, though they would listen with interest to me never seemed to agree. I tried once or twice to explain to able men what I meant by natural selection, but signally failed. What I believe was strictly true is that innumerable well-observed facts were stored in the minds of naturalists ready to take their proper places, as soon as any theory which would receive them was sufficiently explained. Another element in the success of the book was its moderate size, and this I owe to the appearance of Wallace's essay; had I published on the scale in which I began to write in 1856, the book would have been four or five times as large as the Origin, and very few would have had the patience to read it.

I gained much by my delay in publishing from about 1839, when the theory was clearly conceived, to 1859; and I lost nothing by it, for I cared very little whether men attributed most originality to me or Wallace, and his essay no doubt aided in the reception of the theory. I was forestalled in only one important point, which my vanity has always made me regret, namely the explanation by means of the Glacial period of the presence of the same species of plants and of some few animals on distant mountain-summits and in the Arctic regions. This view pleased me so much that I wrote it out in extenso, and it was read by Hooker, some years before E. Forbes published his celebrated memoir on the subject. In the very few points in which we differed, I still think that I was in the right. I have never of course alluded in print to my having independently worked out this view.

Hardly any point gave me so much satisfaction when I was at work on the Origin, as the explanation of the wide difference in many classes between the embryo and the adult animal, and of the close resemblance of the embryos within the same class.[1] No notice of this point was taken, as far as I remember, in the early reviews of the Origin, and I recollect expressing my surprise on this head in a letter to Asa Gray. Within late years several reviewers have given the whole credit of the idea to Fritz Müller and Häckel,[2] who undoubtedly have worked it out much more fully, and in some respects more correctly than I did. I had materials for a whole chapter on the subject, and I ought to have made the discussion longer; for it is clear that I failed to impress my readers; and he who succeeds in doing so deserves in my opinion all the credit.

This leads me to remark that I have almost always been treated honestly by my reviewers, passing over those without scientific knowledge as not worthy of notice. My views have often been grossly misrepresented, bitterly opposed and ridiculed, but this has been generally done as I believe in good faith. I must however except Mr. Mivart, who as an American expressed it in a letter has acted towards me 'like a pettifogger', or as Huxley has said 'like an Old Bailey lawyer.' On the whole I do not doubt that my work has been over and over again greatly overpraised. I rejoice that I have avoided controversies, and this I owe to Lyell, who many years ago in reference to my geological works strongly advised me never to get entangled in a controversy, as it rarely did any good and caused a miserable loss of time and temper.

Whenever I have found out that I have blundered or that my work has been imperfect, and when I have been contemptuously criticised and even when I have been overpraised, so that I have felt mortified, it has been my greatest comfort to say hundreds of times to myself that 'I have worked as hard and as well as I could, and no man can do more than this.' I remember when in Good Success Bay in Tierra del Fuego, thinking, (and I believe that I wrote home to this effect) that I could not employ my life better than in adding a little to natural science. This I have done to the best of my abilities, and critics may say what they like, but they cannot destroy this conviction.

During the two last months of the year 1859 I was fully occupied in preparing a second edition of the Origin, and by an enormous correspondence. On January 7th 1860 I began arranging my notes for my work on the Variation of Animals and Plants under domestication; but it was not published until the beginning of 1868; the delay having been caused partly by frequent illnesses, one of which lasted seven months, and partly by having been tempted to publish on other subjects which at the time interested me more.

On May 15th 1862, my little book on the Fertilisation of Orchids, which cost me ten months work, was published: most of the facts had been slowly accumulated during several previous years. During the summer of 1839 and I believe during the previous summer, I was led to attend to the cross-fertilisation of flowers by the aid of insects, from having come to the conclusion in my speculations on the origin of species, that crossing played an important part in keeping specific forms constant. I attended to the subject more or less during every subsequent summer; and my interest in it was greatly enhanced by having procured and read in November 1841, through the advice of Robert Brown, a copy of C. K. Sprengels wonderful book 'Das entdeckte Geheimnis der Natur'. For some years before 1862 I had specially attended to the fertilisation of our British orchids; and it seemed to me the best plan to prepare as complete a treatise on this group of plants as well as I could, rather than to utilise the great mass of matter which I had slowly collected with respect to other plants. My resolve proved a wise one; for since the appearance of my book, a surprising number of papers and separate works on the fertilisation of all kinds of flowers have appeared; and these are far better done than I could possibly have effected. The merits of poor old Sprengel, so long overlooked, are now fully recognised many years after his death.

During this same year I published in the Journal of the Linnean Society a paper 'On the two forms or dimorphic condition of primula', and during the next five years, five other papers on dimorphic and trimorphic plants. I do not think anything in my scientific life has given me so much satisfaction as making out the meaning of the structure of these plants. I had noticed in 1838 or 1839 the dimorphism of *Linum flavum*, and had at first thought that it was merely a case of unmeaning variability. But on examining the common species of Primula I found that the two forms were much too regular and constant to be thus viewed. I therefore became almost convinced that the common cowslip and primrose were on the high road to become diœcious;—that the short pistil in the one form, and the short stamens in the other form were tending towards abortion. The plants were therefore subjected under this point of view to trial; but as soon as the flowers with short pistils fertilised with pollen from the short stamens, were found to yield more seeds than any other of the four possible unions, the abortion-theory was knocked on the head. After some additional experiment, it became evident that the two forms, though both were perfect hermaphrodites, bore almost the same relation to one another as do the two sexes of an ordinary animal. With Lythrum we have the still more wonderful case of three forms standing in a similar relation to one another. I afterwards found that the offspring from the union of two plants belonging to the same forms presented a close and curious analogy with hybrids from the union of two distinct species.

In the autumn of 1864 I finished a long paper on Climbing Plants and sent it to the Linnean Society. The writing of this paper cost me four months: but I was so unwell when I received the proof-sheets that I was forced to leave them very badly and often obscurely expressed. The paper was little noticed, but when in 1875 it was corrected and published as a separate book it sold well. I was led to take up this subject by reading a short paper by Asa Gray, published in 1858, on the movements of the tendrils of a Cucurbitacean plant. He sent me seeds, and on raising some plants I was so much fascinated and perplexed by the revolving movements of the tendrils and stems, which movements are really very simple though appearing at first very complex, that I procured various other kinds of Climbing Plants, and studied the whole subject. I was all the more attracted to it, from not being at all satisfied with the explanation which Henslow gave us in his Lectures, about Twining plants, namely that they had a natural tendency to grow up in a spire. This explanation proved quite erroneous. Some of the adaptations displayed by Climbing Plants are as beautiful as those by Orchids for ensuring cross-fertilisation.

My Variation of Animals and Plants under domestication was begun, as already stated, in the beginning of 1860, but was not published until the beginning of 1868. It is a big book and cost me four years and two months hard labour. It gives all my observations and an immense number of facts collected from various sources about our domestic productions. In the second volume the causes and laws of variation, inheritance, &c., are discussed, as far as our present state of knowledge permits. Towards the end of the work I give my well-abused hypothesis of Pangenesis. An unverified hypothesis is of little or no value; but if anyone should hereafter be led to make observations by which some such hypothesis could be established, I shall have done good service, as an astonishing number of isolated facts can thus be connected together and rendered intelligible. In 1875 a second and largely corrected edition, which cost me a good deal of labour, was brought out.

My Descent of Man was published in Feb. 1871. As soon as I had become in the year 1837 or 1838 convinced that species were mutable productions, I could not avoid the belief that man must come under the same law. Accordingly I collected notes on the subject for my own satisfaction, and not for a long time with any intention of publishing. Although in the Origin of Species, the derivation of any particular species is never discussed, yet I thought it best, in order that no honourable man should accuse me of concealing my views, to add that by the work in question 'light would be thrown on the origin of man and his history.' It would have been useless and injurious to the success of the book to have paraded without giving any evidence my conviction with respect to his origin. But when I found that many naturalists fully accepted the doctrine of the evolution of species, it seemed to me advisable to work up such notes as I possessed and to publish a special treatise on the origin of man. I was the more glad to do so, as it gave me an opportunity of fully discussing sexual selection, —a subject which had always greatly interested me. This subject, and that of the variation of our domestic productions together with the causes and laws of variation, inheritance, &c., and the intercrossing of Plants are the sole subjects which I have been able to write about in full, so as to use all the materials which I had collected. The Descent of Man took me three years to write, but then as usual some of this time was lost by ill-health, and some was consumed by preparing new editions and other minor works. A second and largely corrected edition of the Descent appeared in 1874.

My book on the Expression of the Emotions in Men and Animals[1] was published in the autumn of 1872. I had intended to give only a chapter on the subject in the Descent of Man, but as soon as I began to put my notes together, I saw that it would require a separate Treatise. My first child[2] was born on December 27th 1839, and I at once commenced to make notes on the first dawn of the various expressions which he exhibited, for I felt convinced, even at this early period, that the most complex and fine shades of expression must all have had a gradual and natural origin. During the summer of the following year, 1840, I read Sir C. Bell's admirable work on Expression, and this greatly increased the interest which I felt in the subject, though I could not at all agree with his belief that various muscles had been specially created for the sake of expression. From this time forward I occasionally attended to the subject, both with respect to man and our domestic animals. My book sold largely; 5267 copies having been disposed of on the day of publication.

In the summer of 1860 I was idling and resting near Hartfield,[3] where two species of Drosera abound; and I noticed that numerous insects had been entrapped by the leaves. I carried home some plants and on giving them insects saw the movements of the tentacles, and this made me think it probable that the insects were caught for some special purpose. Fortunately a crucial test occurred to me, that of placing a large number of leaves in various nitrogenous and non-nitrogenous fluids of equal density; and as soon as I found that the former alone excited energetic movements, it was obvious that here was a fine new field for investigation. During subsequent years, whenever I had leisure I pursued my experiments, and my book on 'Insectivorous Plants' was published July 1875,—that is 16 years after my first observations. The delay in this case, as with all my other books has been a great advantage to me; for a man after a long interval can criticise his own work, almost as well as if it were that of another person. The fact that a plant should secrete when properly excited a fluid containing an acid and ferment, closely analogous to the digestive fluid of an animal, was certainly a remarkable discovery.

During this autumn of 1876 I shall publish on the 'Effects of Cross

and Self Fertilisation in the Vegetable Kingdom.' This book will
form a complement to that on the Fertilisation of Orchids, in which
I showed how perfect were the means for cross-fertilisation, and here
I shall show how important are the results. I was led to make during
eleven years the numerous experiments recorded in this volume by a
mere accidental observation; and indeed it required the accident to be
repeated before my attention was thoroughly aroused to the
remarkable fact that seedlings of self-fertilised parentage are inferior
even in the first generation in height and vigour to seedlings of
cross-fertilised parentage. I hope also to republish a revised edition of
my book on Orchids, and hereafter my papers on dimorphic and
trimorphic plants, together with some additional observations on
allied points which I never have had time to arrange. My strength
will then probably be exhausted, and I shall be ready to exclaim
'nunc dimittis.'

'The Effects of Cross and Self Fertilisation'[1] was published in the
autumn of 1876; and the results there arrived at explain, as I believe,
the endless and wonderful contrivances for the transportal of pollen
from one plant to another of the same species. I now believe, however, chiefly from the observations of Hermann Müller, that I
ought to have insisted more strongly than I did on the many
adaptations for self-fertilisation; though I was well aware of many
such adaptations. A much enlarged Edit. of my Fertilisation of
Orchids was published in 1877.

In this same year 'The Different Forms of Flowers, &c.' appeared,
and in 1880 a 2ᵈ edition. This book consists chiefly of the several
papers on heterostyled flowers, originally published by the Linnean
Socʸ, corrected with much new matter added, together with
observations on some other cases in which the same plant bears two
kinds of flowers. As before remarked no little discovery of mine
ever gave me so much pleasure as the making out the meaning of
heterostyled flowers. The results of crossing such flowers in an
illegitimate manner, I believe to be very important as bearing on the
sterility of hybrids; although these results have been noticed by only
a few persons.

In 1879, I had a translation of Dr. Ernst Krause's life of Erasmus Darwin published, and I added a sketch of his character and habits from materials in my possession. Many persons have been much interested by this little life, and I am surprised that only 800 or 900 copies were sold. Owing to my having accidentally omitted to mention that Dr. Krause had enlarged and corrected his article in German before it was translated, Mr. Samuel Butler abused me with almost insane virulence. How I offended him so bitterly, I have never been able to understand. The subject gave rise to some controversy in the Athenaeum newspaper and Nature. I laid all the documents before some good judges, viz. Huxley, Leslie Stephen, Litchfield, &c., and they were all unanimous that the attack was so baseless that it did not deserve any public answer; for I had already expressed privately my regret to Mr. Butler for my accidental omission. Huxley consoled me by quoting some German lines from Goethe, who had been attacked by someone, to the effect 'that every Whale has its Louse.'

In 1880 I published, with Frank's[1] assistance, our 'Power of Movement in Plants'.[2] This was a tough piece of work. The book bears somewhat the same relation to my little book on Climbing Plants, which 'Cross-Fertilisation' did to the 'Fertilisation of Orchids'; for in accordance with the principles of evolution it was impossible to account for climbing plants having been developed in so many widely different groups, unless all kinds of plants possess some slight power of movement of an analogous kind. This I proved to be the case, and I was further led to a rather wide generalisation, viz., that the great and important classes of movement, excited by light, the attraction of gravity, &c., are all modified forms of the fundamental movement of circumnutation. It has always pleased me to exalt plants in the scale of organised beings; and I therefore felt an especial pleasure in showing how many and what admirably well adapted movements the tip of a root possesses.

I have now (May 1st 1881) sent to the printers the M.S of a little book on 'The Formation of Vegetable Mould, through the action of worms'.[3] This is a subject of but small importance; and I know not whether it will interest any readers, but it has interested me. It is the completion of a short paper read before the Geological Society more than 40 years ago, and has revived old geological thoughts.

I have now mentioned all the books which I have published, and these have been the mile-stones in my life, so that little remains to be said. I am not conscious of any change in my mind during the last 30 years, excepting in one point presently to be mentioned; nor indeed could any change have been expected unless one of general deterioration. But my Father lived to his 83.^{d} years with his mind as lively as ever it was, and all his faculties undimmed; and I hope that I may die before mine fails to a sensible extent. I think that I have become a little more skilful in guessing right explanations and in devising experimental tests; but this may probably be the result of mere practice and of a larger store of knowledge. I have as much difficulty as ever in expressing myself clearly and concisely; and this difficulty has caused me a very great loss of time; but it has had the compensating advantage of forcing me to think long and intently about every sentence, and thus I have been often led to see errors in reasoning and in my own observations or those of others. There seems to be a sort of fatility in my mind leading me to put at first my statement and proposition in a wrong or awkward form. Formerly I used to think about my sentences before writing them down; but for several years I have found that it saves time to scribble in a vile hand whole pages as quickly as I possibly can, contracting half the words; and then correct deliberately. Sentences thus scribbled down are often better ones than I could have written deliberately.

Having said this much about my manner of writing, I will add that with my larger books I spend a good deal of time over the general arrangement of the matter. I first make the rudest outline in two or three pages, and then a larger one in several pages, a few words or one word standing for a whole discussion or series of facts. Each of these headings is again enlarged and often transformed before I begin to write in extenso. As in several of my books facts observed by others have been very extensively used, and as I have always had several quite distinct subjects in hand at the same time, I may mention that I keep from 30 to 40 large portfolios, in cabinets with labelled shelves, into which I can at once put a detached reference or memorandum. I have bought many books and at their ends I make an index of all the facts that concern my work; or if the book is not my own, write out a separate abstract, and of such abstracts I have a large drawer full. Before beginning on any subject I look to all the short indexes and make a general and classified index, and by taking the one or more proper portfolios I have all the information collected during my life ready for use.

I have said that in one respect my mind has changed during the last 20 or 30 years. Up to the age of thirty, or beyond it, poetry of many kinds, such as the works of Milton, Gray, Byron, Wordsworth, Coleridge and Shelley, gave me great pleasure, and even as a schoolboy I took intense delight in Shakespeare especially in the historical plays. I have also said that formerly Pictures gave me considerable, and music very great delight. But now for many years I cannot endure to read a line of poetry: I have tried lately to read Shakespeare and found it so intolerably dull that it nauseated me. I have also almost lost any taste for pictures or music.—Music generally sets me thinking too energetically on what I have been at work on, instead of giving me pleasure. I retain some taste for fine scenery, but it does not cause me the exquisite delight which it formerly did. On the other hand, novels which are works of the imagination, though not of a very high order, have been for years a wonderful relief and pleasure to me, and I often bless all novelists. A surprising number have been read aloud to me, and I like all if moderately good, and if they do not end unhappily—against which a law ought to be passed. A novel, according to my taste, does not come into the first class, unless it contains some person whom one can thoroughly love, and if it be a pretty woman all the better.

This curious and lamentable loss of the higher aesthetic tastes is all the odder, as books on history, biographies and travels (independently of any scientific facts which they may contain), and essays on all sorts of subjects interest me as much as ever they did. My mind seems to

83

have become a kind of machine for grinding general laws out of large collections of facts, but why this should have caused the atrophy of that part of the brain alone, on which the higher tastes depend, I cannot conceive. A man with a mind more highly organised or better constituted than mine, would not I suppose have thus suffered; and if I had to live my life again I would have made a rule to read some poetry and listen to some music at least once every week; for perhaps the parts of my brain now atrophied could thus have been kept active through use. The loss of these tastes is a loss of happiness, and may possibly be injurious to the intellect, and more probably to the moral character by enfeebling the emotional part of our nature.

My books have sold largely in England, have been translated into many languages and passed through several editions in foreign countries. I have heard it said that the success of a work abroad is the best test of its enduring value. I doubt whether this is at all trust-worthy, but judged by this standard my name ought to last for a few years. Therefore it may be worth while for me to try to analyse the mental qualities and the conditions on which my success has depended; though I am aware that no man can do this correctly. I have no great quickness of apprehension or wit which is so remarkable in some clever men, for instance Huxley. I am therefore a poor critic: a paper or book, when first read, generally excites my admiration, and it is only after considerable reflection that I perceive the weak points. My power to follow a long and purely abstract train of thought is very limited; I should, therefore, never have succeeded with meta-physics or mathematics. My memory is extensive, yet hazy: it suffices to make me cautious by vaguely telling me that I have observed or read something opposed to the conclusion which I am drawing, or on the other hand in favour of it; and after a time I can generally recollect where to search for my authority. So poor in one sense is my memory, that I have never been able to remember for more than a few days a single date or a line of poetry. Some of my critics have said, 'Oh, he is a good observer but has no power of reasoning.' I do not think that this can be true, for the Origin of

Species is one long argument from the beginning to the end, and it has convinced not a few able men. No one could have written it without having some power of reasoning. I have a fair share of invention and of common sense or judgment, such as every fairly successful lawyer or doctor must have, but not I believe in any higher degree.

On the favourable side of the balance I think that I am superior to the common run of men in noticing things which easily escape attention, and in observing them carefully. My industry has been nearly as great as it could have been in the observation and collection of facts. What is far more important my love of natural science has been steady and ardent. This pure love has however been much aided by the ambition to be esteemed by my fellow naturalists. From my early youth I have had the strongest desire to understand or explain whatever I observed,—that is to group all facts under some general laws. These causes combined have given me the patience to reflect or ponder for any number of years over any unexplained problem. As far as I can judge, I am not apt to follow blindly the lead of other men. I have steadily endeavoured to keep my mind free, so as to give up any hypothesis, however much beloved (and I cannot resist forming one on every subject) as soon as facts are shown to be opposed to it. Indeed I have had no choice but to act in this manner, for with the exception of the Coral Reefs I cannot remember a single first-formed hypothesis which had not after a time to be given up or greatly modified. This has naturally led me to distrust greatly deductive reasoning in the mixed sciences. On the other hand I am not very sceptical,—a frame of mind which I believe to be injurious to the progress of science; a good deal of scepticism in a scientific man is advisable to avoid much loss of time; for I have met with not a few men, who I feel sure have often thus been deterred from experiment or observations, which would have proved directly or indirectly serviceable.

In illustration, I will give the oddest case which I have known. A gentleman (who as I afterwards heard was a good local botanist) wrote to me from the Eastern counties that the seeds or beans in the common field-bean had this year everywhere grown on the wrong side of the pod. I wrote back, asking for further information, as I did not understand what was meant; but I did not receive any answer for a long time. I then saw in two newspapers, one published in Kent and the other in Yorkshire, paragraphs stating that it was a most remarkable fact that the beans this year had all grown on the wrong side. So I thought that there must be some foundation for so general a statement. Accordingly I went to my gardener, an old Kentish man, and asked him whether he had heard anything about it; and he answered 'Oh no Sir, it must be a mistake, for the beans grow on the wrong side only on Leap-year, and this is not Leap-year.' I then asked him how they grew on common years and how on leap-years, but soon found out that he knew absolutely nothing of how they grew at any time; but he stuck to his belief. After a time I heard from my first informant, who with many apologies said that he should not have written to me had he not heard the statement from several intelligent farmers; but that he had since spoken again to every one of them, and not one knew in the least what he had himself meant. So that here a belief—if indeed a statement with no definite idea attached to it can be called a belief—had spread over almost the whole of England without any vestige of evidence. I have known in the course of my life only three intentionally falsified statements, and one of these may have been a hoax (and there have been several scientific hoaxes) which, however, took in an American Agricultural Journal. It related to the formation in Holland of a new breed of oxen by the crossing of distinct species of Bos (some of which I happen to know are sterile together), and the author had the impudence to state that he had corresponded with me and that I had been deeply impressed with the importance of his results. The article was sent to me by the editor of an English Agricult. Journal, asking for my opinion before republishing it.

A second case was an account of several varieties raised by the author from several species of Primula, which had spontaneously yielded a full complement of seed, although the parent-plants had been carefully protected from the access of insects. This account was

Thomas Henry Huxley, 1857

H.M.S. Rattlesnake leaving anchorage on 6 June 1848: pencil sketch by W. Brierly

published before I had discovered the meaning of heterostylism,[1] and the whole statement must have been fraudulent, or there was neglect in excluding insects so gross as to be scarcely credible.

The third case was more curious: Mr. Huth published in his book on consanguineous marriage some long extracts from a Belgian author, who stated that he had interbred rabbits in the closest manner for very many generations without the least injurious effects. The account was published in a most respectable Journal, that of the R. Medical Soc. of Belgium; but I could not avoid feeling doubts,— I hardly know why, except that there were no accidents of any kind, and my experience in breeding animals made me think this improbable.

So with much hesitation I wrote to Prof. Van Beneden asking him whether the author was a trustworthy man. I soon heard in answer that the Society had been greatly shocked by discovering that the whole account was a fraud. The writer had been publicly challenged in the Journal to say where he had resided and kept his large stock of rabbits while carrying on his experiments, which must have consumed several years, and no answer could be extracted from him. I informed poor Mr. Huth, that the account which formed the corner-stone of his argument was fraudulent; and he in the most honourable manner immediately had a slip printed to this effect to be inserted in all future copies of his book which might be sold.

My habits are methodical, and this has been of not a little use for my particular line of work. Lastly, I have had ample leisure from not having to earn my own bread. Even ill-health, though it has annihilated several years of my life, has saved me from the distractions of society and amusement.

Therefore, my success as a man of science, whatever this may have amounted to, has been determined, as far as I can judge, by complex and diversified mental qualities and conditions. Of these the most important have been—the love of science—unbounded patience in long reflecting over any subject—industry in observing and collecting facts—and a fair share of invention as well as of common sense. With such moderate abilities as I possess, it is truly surprising that thus I should have influenced to a considerable extent the beliefs of scientific men on some important points.

August 3ʳᵈ 1876

This sketch of my life was begun about May 28th. at Hopedene,[1] and since then I have written for nearly an hour on most afternoons.

THOMAS HENRY HUXLEY

Notebook: 'Thoughts and Doings'[1]

===

SEPTEMBER 29 1840. Remember to make a galvanic battery with lead or iron on the first opportunity—Also to try the experiment of a simple galvanic current—having syrup instead of sulphate of copper and dilute sulphuric acid to act on the zinc—Might not crystallised carbon be obtained thus?

October 1—Went to Hinckley[2]

—— 5—Began speculating on the cause of colours at sunset—Has any explanation of them even been attempted? There is no necessity for supposing the atmosphere to be liquefied if it has an internal reflecting angle as it must have, it is sufficient. Does not the colour of the sky at sunrise and sunset arise from the reflexion of the rays of light from some liquid? perhaps liquefied air in the upper cold regions.

In this case the colours would appear in this order, from the sun, red, orange, yellow, green blue—red is seen nearest the sun because being refracted least, it strikes on the reflecting surface at the greatest angle and reaches the eye of the spectator first—Of course all these effects may be much modified by the passage of the rays through transparent clouds such as those mentioned by Humboldt—through masses of vapour also and by unequal heating of the atmosphere.

October 19. Saw an aurora borealis between 7 and 8 P.M. it appeared as a mass of milk white light in the horizon (N.W.) from whence extended 5 or 6 streamers to the zenith—it passed to the north as I watched and when I last saw it the streamers passed through Ursa Major—A brilliant shooting star crossed one of the streamers—there had been a very high wind all day.

[October] 25th at Hinckley—read Dr. S. Smith[3] on the Divine Government—Agree with him partly—I should say that a general belief in his doctrines would have a very injurious effect on morals. [God help you goose! 1845]

November 1st. tried an electrolyte experiment.

—— 2—Had a long talk with my mother and father about the right to make Dissenters pay church rates—and whether there ought to be any Establishment—I maintained that there ought not in both cases—I wonder what will be my opinions 10 years hence? I think *now* that it is against all laws of justice to force men to support a church with whose opinions they cannot conscientiously agree— The argument that the rate is so small is very fallacious. It is as much a sacrifice of principle to do a little wrong as to do a great one— [November] 5th. Tried proposition No. 2 (Sept. 29th.) carbon is deposited on the copper plate but not crystallised, perhaps this arises from the shortness of the time the experiment has taken—

Perhaps with a thicker division of plaster I might obtain different results—

[November] 22nd. Sunday. Hinckley. Had a long argument with Mr. May[1] on the nature of the soul and the difference between it and matter. I maintained that it cannot be proved that matter is *essentially* —as to its base—different from soul. Mr. M. wittily said, soul was the perspiration of matter—We cannot find the absolute basis of matter, we only know it by its properties, neither know we the soul in any other way—Cogito, ergo sum[2]—is the only thing we *certainly* know.

Why may not soul and matter be of the same substance (i.e. basis whereon to fix qualities for we cannot suppose a quality to exist per se —it must have a something to qualify) but with different qualities— Let us suppose then an Eon—a something with no quality but that of existence—this Eon endued with all the intelligent mental qualities and that in the highest degree—is God—This combination of intelligence with existence we may suppose to have existed from eternity—

At the creation we may suppose that a portion of the Eon was separated from the intelligence and it was ordained—it became a natural law—that it should have the properties of gravitation &c., that is that it should give to man the idea of those properties—The Eon in this state is matter in the abstract. Matter then is Eon in the

simplest form in which it possesses qualities appreciable by the senses
—Out of this matter by the superimposition of fresh qualities was
made all things that are—

1841 January 7 came to Rotherhithe—

June 20th. What have I done in the way of acquiring knowledge
since January?

Projects begun—

1. German ⎫
2. Italian ⎬ to be learnt

3. To read Muller's Physiology[1]

4. To prepare for the Matriculation Examination at London University which requires a knowledge of:

a. Algebra—Geometry   Did not begin

b. Natural Philosophy   to read for this

c. Chemistry   till April 9

d. Greek—Latin

e. English History down to end of 17th century

f. Ancient History

g. English Grammar

5. To make copious notes of all things I read—

Projects completed—

1. partly— 2. not at all

3. 5. stuck to these pretty closely

4. e. read as far as Henry III in Hume[2]

a. Evolution and involution

b. refraction of light—polarisation partly

c. laws of combination—must read them over again

d. f. g. nothing.

I must get on faster than this—I *must* adopt a fixed plan of studies
for unless this is done I find time slips away without knowing it—
and let me remember this—that it is better to read a little and
thoroughly than cram a crude indigestible mass into my head—
though it be great in quantity—[This is about the only resolution I
have ever stuck to! 1845]

[Well do I remember how in that little narrow surgery I used to work morning after morning and evening after evening—that insufferably dry and profitless book Hume's History. How I worked against hope through the series of thefts robberies and throat cutting in those three first volumes and how at length I gave up the task in utter disgust and despair.

Macintosh's[1] History on the other hand I remember reading with great pleasure and also Guizot's[2] Civilisation in Europe—The scientific theoretical form of the latter especially pleased me—but the want of sufficient knowledge to test his conclusions was a great drawback. 1845.]

Week June 20 to 27

Tuesday Thursday—Physiology

Monday, Wednesday, Friday, chronological abstract of reigns of Henry III, Edward I, II, and III

Evenings—14 Theorems—Arithmetical Propositions

Saturday—Read over Atomic Theory and Laws of combination and Electricity—Turner[3] and Manuel—An hour every afternoon for German.

[Quotations from Lessing, Goethe, and Iselin.]

Week June 27 to July 4

Monday, Wednesday (out), Friday—chronological abstracts and reading Edward III—Review—in part

Tuesday, Thursday (ill) Physiology

Evenings—10 theorems and review Geom. propositions and review —German

What with going out and being unwell have been very idle this week—

Week July 4 to 11—

Monday, Wednesday, Friday—Chronological abstracts of Richard II Henry IV and Henry 5

Tuesday, Thursday, (Physiology), abstract pages 231 to 244, read to end of Cap. III

Geometry—12 theorems and reviews.

Algebra—Addition, subtraction, multiplication and division with *reasons for the rules.*

German. Loben—learn conjugations of—Translate—
  Week August 2 to 9
History (every morning)—Henry IV, V and VI. Read abstract.
German (afternoons)—Translate 'Die Ideale'—
Mathematics (evenings)—1st part of Infinite series—Equations of one
  or two unknowns—
Did nothing worth mentioning in the latter part of July, [illegible]
out from 15 to 19th.—19th. to 26th. engaged in making an electro-
magnet. 26th. to 31st. read 'Guizot's History of Civilisation' an
excellent work—very tough reading though.
September 27th. 1841—to October 4
Laid out for this week
A. (history)—Guizot on Feudalism—Robertson[1] on same—finish
  Hume volume iii.
B. (mathematics)—Review 20 Theorems, begin the Geometry of
  Circles and go through Proportions and Progressions (Manuel).
C. (German)—get up in German adjectives.
Monday a. Read Robertson 7 with 8—Review Guizot, Edward IV
          Richard III
        b. Theorem X
        c. German adjectives;
Miscellaneous—Became acquainted with constitution of the French
  chambre des députés and their parties—
Tuesday—Henry VII
        Proportions

1842—January 30th.
Sunday Evening
  I have for some time past been pondering over a Classification of
Knowledge. My scheme is—to divide all knowledge in the first
place into two grand divisions.
I. Objective—that for which a man is indebted to the external world,
and
II. Subjective—that which he has acquired or may acquire by inward
contemplation.

Metaphysics comes immediately of course under the first[1] head—that is to say the relations of mind to itself—of this mathematics and logic together with theology are branches—

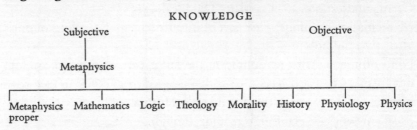

KNOWLEDGE

Subjective						Objective	

Metaphysics

Metaphysics proper	Mathematics	Logic	Theology	Morality	History	Physiology	Physics

I am in doubt under which head to put morality for I cannot determine exactly in my own mind whether morality can exist independent of others—whether the idea of morality could ever have arisen in the mind of an isolated being or not—I am rather inclined to the opinion that it is objective.

Under the head of Objective Knowledge comes firstly Physics—including the whole body of the relations of inanimate unorganised bodies—2 Physiology—including the structure and functions of animal bodies including language and Psychology, thirdly comes History.

The object for which I have attempted to form an arrangement of knowledge is that I may test the amount of my own acquirement. I shall form an extensive list of subjects on this plan and as I acquire any one of them I shall strike it off the list. May the list soon get black! Though at present I shall hardly be able I am afraid, to spot the paper—

[a Prophecy! a Prophecy! 1845]

April 1842—

[Quotations from Carlyle's *Miscellaneous Writings*, 'Characteristics' (Edinburgh Review 1831)]

June 1842

[diagram of electrical experiment]

I observe that on making the experiment in the figure, the Galvanometer needle is deflected. This may arise from one of three causes. First the circuit being completed partially through p p though this is extremely improbable. Secondly from an induction similar to that of electricity. Thirdly from an induction similar to that of a wire through which a current is passing upon another wire.

The first supposition cannot be true because firstly the secondary current would in that case be stronger when connexion is broken at A whereas in that case all effect ceases—secondly because the secondary current is in an opposite direction to the primary.

(2) The second view appears to me the most probable—to wit that the liquid (acid and s[ulphate of] copper) acts as a sort of dielectric (?) precisely similar to a plate of air through which induction ordinary is going on—For if a piece of copper be placed like d e, the extremity d becomes covered with copper and extremity e dissolves off—Here there is a polarisation precisely similar to that of a plate of metal insulated and placed between an inducteous and inductive body. In the case of the experiment itself I imagine that the platinum plates are in precisely the same state that two metal plates connected by a wire would be if placed as above. Would not in this case one of them become entirely positive and the other entirely negative

I would suppose then that particles [. . .]
Try whether connecting the zinc with the Plate in its cell through the galvanometer will have any effect.

Modern Poets of whom I know too little
Robert Browning, Author of Paracelsus, Sordello, &c.[1]
P. J. Bailey, Author of Festus[2]
Thomas Wade
Monckton Milnes
Hartley Coleridge
Horne

October 1845

I have found a singular pleasure—having accidentally raked this Büchlein from a corner of my desk—in looking over these scraps of notices of my past existence. An illustration of S. Pauls saying that a man has but to write down his yesterdays doings and forthwith they appear surrounded with a poetic halo.

But after all these are but the top skimmings of these five years living—I hardly care to look back into the seething depths of the working and boiling mass that lay beneath all this froth and indeed I hardly know whether I could give myself any clear account of it— Remembrances of Physical and Mental pain—absence of sympathy and thence a choking up of such few ideas as I did form clearly within my own mind—

Grief too—yet at the misfortunes of others—for I have had few properly my own—so much the worse for in that case I might have said or done somewhat but here was powerless.

Oh Tom trouble not thyself about sympathy. Thou has two stout legs and young, wherefore need a staff? Furthermore it is twenty minutes past two—and time to go to bed.

Büchlein it will be long before my secretiveness remains so quiet again—make the most of what thou hast got.

Passage from a Journal[1]

[A glimpse of his grief at the misfortunes of others is given by the following, relating to the early years of his medical studies, contemporary with 'Thoughts and Doings'. The scene is Rotherhithe]

I saw strange things there—among the rest, people who came to me for medical aid, and who were really suffering from nothing but slow starvation. I have not forgotten—am not likely to forget so long as memory holds—a visit to a sick girl in a wretched garret where two or three other women, one a deformed woman, sister of my patient, were busy shirt-making. After due examination, even my small medical knowledge sufficed to show that my patient was merely in want of some better food than the bread and bad tea on which these people were living. I said so as gently as I could, and the sister turned upon me with a kind of choking passion. Pulling out of her pocket a few pence and halfpence, and holding them out, 'That is all I get for six-and-thirty hours' work, and you talk about giving her proper food'.

Well, I left that to pursue my medical studies, and it so happened the shortest way between the school which I attended and the library of the College of Surgeons, where my spare hours were largely spent, lay through certain courts and alleys, Vinegar Yard and others, which are now nothing like what they were then. Nobody would have found robbing me a profitable employment in those days, and I used to walk through these wretched dens without let or hindrance. Alleys nine or ten feet wide, I suppose, with tall houses full of squalid drunken men and women, and the pavement strewed with still more squalid children. The place of air was taken by a steam of filthy exhalations; and the only relief to the general dull apathy was a roar of words—filthy and brutal beyond imagination—between close-packed neighbours, occasionally ending in a general row. All this almost within hearing of the traffic of the Strand, within easy reach of the wealth and plenty of the city.

I used to wonder sometimes why these people did not sally forth in mass and get a few hours' eating and drinking and plunder to their hearts' content, before the police could stop and hang a few of them. But the poor wretches had not the heart even for that. As a slight, wiry Liverpool detective once said to me when I asked him how it was he managed to deal with such hulking ruffians as we were among, 'Lord bless you, sir, drink and disease leave nothing in them'.

'Autobiography'

[February 1889]

'MY DEAR MR. ENGEL,—

'You really are the most pertinaciously persuasive of men. When you first wrote to me, I said I would have nothing whatever to do with anything you might please to say about me, that I had a profound objection to write about myself, and that I could not see what business the public had with my private life. I think I even expressed to you my complete sympathy with Dr. Johnson's desire to take Boswell's life when he heard of the latter's occupation with his biography.

'Undeterred by all this, you put before me the alternative of issuing something that may be all wrong, unless I furnish you with something authoritative; I do not say all right, because autobiographies are essentially works of fiction, whatever biographies may be. So I yield, and send you what follows, in the hope that those who find it to be mere egotistical gossip will blame you and not me.

                              'I am
                                   'Yours faithfully,
                                        'T. H. HUXLEY.'

I was born about eight o'clock in the morning on the 4th of May, 1825, at Ealing, which was, at that time, as quiet a little country village as could be found within half a dozen miles of Hyde Park Corner. Now it is a suburb of London with, I believe, 30,000 inhabitants. I am not aware that any portents preceded my arrival in this world; but, in my childhood, I remember hearing a traditional account of the manner in which I lost the chance of an endowment of great practical value. The windows of my mother's room were open, in consequence of the unusual warmth of the weather. For the same reason, probably, a neighbouring bee-hive had swarmed, and the new colony, pitching on the window-sill, was making its way into the room when the horrified nurse shut down the sash. If that

well-meaning woman had only abstained from her ill-timed inter-
ference, the swarm might have settled on my lips, and I should have
been endowed with that mellifluous eloquence which, in this country,
leads far more surely than worth, capacity, or honest work, to the
highest places in Church and State. But the opportunity was lost,
and I have been obliged to content myself through life with saying
what I mean in the plainest of plain language; than which, I suppose,
there is no habit more ruinous to a man's prospects of advancement.
Why I was christened Thomas Henry I do not know; but it is a
curious chance that my parents should have fixed for my usual
denomination upon the name of that particular Apostle with whom
I have always felt most sympathy. Physically and mentally I am the
son of my mother[1] so completely—even down to peculiar movements
of the hands, which made their appearance in me as I reached the age
she had when I noticed them—that I can hardly find any trace of my
father[2] in myself, except an inborn faculty for drawing, which
unfortunately, in my case, has never been cultivated; a hot temper;
and that amount of tenacity of purpose, which unfriendly observers
sometimes call obstinacy.

My mother was a slender brunette, of an emotional and energetic
temperament, and possessed of the most piercing black eyes I ever
saw in a woman's head. With no more education than other women
of the middle classes in her day, she had an excellent mental capacity.
Her most distinguishing characteristic, however, was rapidity of
thought. If one ventured to suggest that she had not taken much time
to arrive at any conclusion, she would say, 'I cannot help it, things
flash across me.' That peculiarity has been passed on to me in full
strength; it has often stood me in good stead; it has sometimes played
me sad tricks, and it has always been a danger. But after all, if my
time were to come over again, there is nothing I would less willingly
part with than my inheritance of mother wit.

I have next to nothing to say about my childhood. In later years,
my mother, looking at me almost reproachfully, would sometimes
say, 'Ah! you were such a pretty boy!' whence I had no difficulty in
concluding that I had not fulfilled my early promise in the matter

of looks. In fact, I have a distinct recollection of certain curls, of which I was vain, and of a conviction that I closely resembled that handsome courtly gentleman, Sir Herbert Oakley,[1] who was vicar of our parish, and who was as a god to us country folk, because he was occasionally visited by the then Prince George of Cambridge. I remember turning my pinafore wrong side forwards, in order to represent a surplice, and preaching to my mother's maids in the kitchen, as nearly as possible in Sir Herbert's manner, one Sunday morning when the rest of the family were at church. That is the earliest indication I can call to mind of the strong clerical affinities which my friend Mr. Herbert Spencer has always ascribed to me, though I fancy they have for the most part remained in a latent state.

My regular school training was of the briefest, perhaps fortunately, for though my way of life has made me acquainted with all sorts and conditions of men, from the highest to the lowest, I deliberately affirm that the society I fell into at school was the worst I have ever known. We boys were average lads, with much the same inherent capacity for good and evil as any others; but the people who were set over us cared about as much for our intellectual and moral welfare as if they were baby farmers. We were left to the operation of the struggle for existence among ourselves, and bullying was the least of the ill practices current among us. Almost the only cheerful reminiscence in connection with the place, which arises in my mind, is that of a battle I had with one of my classmates, who had bullied me until I could stand it no longer. I was a very slight lad, but there was a wild-cat element in me which, when roused, made up for lack of weight, and I licked my adversary effectually. However, one of my first experiences of the extremely rough-and-ready nature of Justice, as exhibited by the course of things in general, arose out of the fact that I, the victor, had a black eye, while he, the vanquished, had none; so that I got into disgrace, and he did not. We made it up, and thereafter I was unmolested. One of the greatest shocks I ever received in my life was to be told, a dozen years afterwards, by the groom who brought me my horse, in a stable-yard in Sydney, that he was my quondam antagonist. He had a long story of family

Samuel Wilberforce, Bishop of Oxford and Winchester

T. H. Huxley

Mrs. T. H. Huxley

misfortune to account for his position; but at that time it was necessary to deal very cautiously with mysterious strangers in New South Wales, and on inquiry I found that the unfortunate young man had not only been 'sent out,' but had undergone more than one colonial conviction.

As I grew older, my great desire was to be a mechanical engineer, but the Fates were against this; and, while very young, I commenced the study of Medicine under a medical brother-in-law.[1] But, though the Institute of Mechanical Engineers would certainly not own me, I am not sure that I have not, all along, been a sort of mechanical engineer *in partibus infidelium*. I am now occasionally horrified to think how very little I ever knew or cared about Medicine as the art of healing. The only part of my professional course which really and deeply interested me was Physiology, which is the mechanical engineering of living machines; and, notwithstanding that natural science has been my proper business, I am afraid there is very little of the genuine naturalist in me. I never collected anything, and species work was always a burden to me; what I cared for was the architectural and engineering part of the business, the working out the wonderful unity of plan in the thousands and thousands of diverse living constructions, and the modifications of similar apparatuses to serve diverse ends. The extraordinary attraction I felt towards the study of the intricacies of living structure nearly proved fatal to me at the outset. I was a mere boy—I think between thirteen and fourteen years of age—when I was taken by some older student friends of mine to the first post mortem examination I ever attended. All my life I have been most unfortunately sensitive to the disagreeables which attend anatomical pursuits; but on this occasion, my curiosity overpowered all other feelings, and I spent two or three hours in gratifying it. I did not cut myself, and none of the ordinary symptoms of dissection poison supervened, but poisoned I was somehow, and I remember sinking into a strange state of apathy. By way of a last chance I was sent to the care of some good, kind people,[2] friends of my father's, who lived in a farmhouse in the heart of Warwickshire. I remember staggering from my bed to the window on the bright spring morning after my arrival, and throwing open the casement. Life seemed to come back on the wings of the breeze; and, to this day, the faint odour of wood-smoke, like that which floated across the farmyard in the early morning, is as good to me as the 'sweet south upon a bed of violets.' I soon recovered; but for years I suffered from occasional paroxysms of internal pain, and from that time my constant friend, hypochondriacal dyspepsia, commenced his half century of co-tenancy of my fleshly tabernacle.

Looking back on my 'Lehrjahre,' I am sorry to say that I do not think that any account of my doings as a student would tend to edification. In fact, I should distinctly warn ingenuous youth to avoid imitating my example. I worked extremely hard when it pleased me, and when it did not (which was a very frequent case) I was extremely idle (unless making caricatures of one's pastors and masters is to be called a branch of industry), or else wasted my energies in wrong directions. I read everything I could lay hands upon, including novels, and took up all sorts of pursuits, to drop them again quite as speedily. No doubt it was very largely my own fault, but the only instruction from which I ever obtained the proper effect of education was that which I received from Mr. Wharton Jones, who was the Lecturer on Physiology at the Charing Cross School of Medicine. The extent and precision of his knowledge impressed me greatly, and the severe exactness of his method of lecturing was quite to my taste. I do not know that I have ever felt so much respect for anybody before or since. I worked hard to obtain his approbation, and he was extremely kind and helpful to the youngster who, I am afraid, took up more of his time than he had any right to do. It was he who suggested the publication of my first scientific paper[1]—a very little one—in the *Medical Gazette* of 1845, and most kindly corrected the literary faults which abounded in it, short as it was; for at that time, and for many years afterwards, I detested the trouble of writing, and would take no pains over it.

It was in the early spring of 1846 that, having finished my obligatory medical studies, and passed the first M.B. examination at the London University (though I was still too young to qualify at the

College of Surgeons), I was talking to a fellow-student—the present eminent physician, Sir Joseph Fayrer—and wondering what I should do to meet the imperative necessity for earning my own bread, when my friend suggested that I should write to Sir William Burnett, at that time Director-General for the Medical Service of the Navy, for an appointment. I thought this rather a strong thing to do, as Sir William was personally unknown to me, but my cheery friend would not listen to my scruples, so I went to my lodgings and wrote the best letter I could devise. A few days afterwards I received the usual official circular of acknowledgment, but at the bottom there was written an instruction to call at Somerset House on such a day. I thought that looked like business, so, at the appointed time, I called and sent in my card, while I waited in Sir William's ante-room. He was a tall, shrewd-looking old gentleman, with a broad Scotch accent—and I think I see him now as he entered with my card in his hand. The first thing he did was to return it, with the frugal reminder that I should probably find it useful on some other occasion. The second was to ask whether I was an Irishman. I suppose the air of modesty about my appeal must have struck him. I satisfied the Director-General that I was English to the backbone, and he made some inquiries as to my student career, finally desiring me to hold myself ready for examination. Having passed this, I was in Her Majesty's Service, and entered on the books of Nelson's old ship *Victory*, for duty at Haslar Hospital, about a couple of months after I made my application.

My official chief at Haslar was a very remarkable person—the late Sir John Richardson, an excellent naturalist, and far-famed as an indomitable Arctic traveller. He was a silent, reserved man outside the circle of his family and intimates; and, having a full share of youthful vanity, I was extremely disgusted to find that 'Old John,' as we irreverent youngsters called him, took not the slightest notice of my worshipful self, either the first time I attended him, as it was my duty to do, or for some weeks afterwards. I am afraid to think of the lengths to which my tongue might have run on the subject of the churlishness of the chief, who was in truth one of the kindest-hearted and most considerate of men. But one day, as I was crossing the Hospital square, Sir John stopped me, and heaped coals of fire on my head by telling me that he had tried to get me one of the resident appointments, much coveted by the assistant-surgeons, but that the Admiralty had put in another man. 'However,' said he, 'I mean to keep you here till I can get you something you will like,' and turned upon his heel without waiting for the thanks I stammered out. That explained how it was I had not been packed off to the West Coast of Africa, like some of my juniors, and why, eventually, I remained altogether seven months at Haslar.

After a long interval, during which 'Old John' ignored my existence almost as completely as before, he stopped me again as we met in a casual way, and describing the service on which the *Rattlesnake* was likely to be employed, said that Captain Owen Stanley,[1] who was to command the ship, had asked him to recommend an assistant-surgeon who knew something of science; would I like that? Of course I jumped at the offer. 'Very well, I give you leave; go to London at once and see Captain Stanley.' I went, saw my future commander, who was very civil to me and promised to ask that I should be appointed to his ship, as in due time I was. It is a singular thing that, during the few months of my stay at Haslar, I had among my messmates two future Directors-General of the Medical Service of the Navy (Sir Alexander Armstrong and Sir John Watt-Reid), with the present President of the College of Physicians and my kindest of doctors, Sir Andrew Clark. Life on board Her Majesty's ships in those days was a very different affair from what it is now; and ours was exceptionally rough, as we were often many months without receiving letters or seeing any civilised people but ourselves. In exchange, we had the interest of being about the last voyagers, I suppose, to whom it could be possible to meet with people who knew nothing of fire-arms—as we did on the South Coast of New Guinea—and of making acquaintance with a variety of interesting savage and semi-civilised people. But, apart from experience of this kind, and the opportunities offered for scientific work, to me, personally, the cruise was extremely valuable. It was good for me to live under sharp discipline; to be down on the realities of existence by living on bare necessaries; to find out how extremely well worth living life seemed to be, when one woke up from a night's rest on a soft plank, with the sky for canopy and cocoa and weevilly biscuit the sole prospect for breakfast; and more especially to learn to work for the sake of what I got for myself out of it, even if it all went to the bottom and I along with it. My brother officers were as good fellows as sailors ought to be and generally are; but, naturally, they neither knew nor cared anything about my pursuits, nor understood why I should be so zealous in pursuit of the objects which my friends the Middies christened 'Buffons,' after the title conspicuous on a volume of the 'Suites à Buffon,' which stood on my shelf in the chart room.

During the four years of our absence, I sent home communication after communication to the 'Linnean Society,' with the same result as that obtained by Noah when he sent the raven out of his ark. Tired at last of hearing nothing about them, I determined to do or die, and, in 1849, I drew up a more elaborate paper[1] and forwarded it to the Royal Society. This was my dove, if I had only known it. But owing to the movements of the ship, I heard nothing of that either, until my return to England in the latter end of the year 1850, when I found that it was printed and published, and that a huge packet of separate copies awaited me. When I hear some of my young friends complain of want of sympathy and encouragement, I am inclined to think that my naval life was not the least valuable part of my education.

Three years after my return were occupied by a battle between my scientific friends on the one hand, and the Admiralty on the other, as to whether the latter ought, or ought not, to act up to the spirit of a pledge they had given to encourage officers who had done scientific work, by contributing to the expense of publishing mine. At last, the Admiralty, getting tired, I suppose, cut short the discussion by ordering me to join a ship. Which thing I declined to do, and as Rastignac, in the Père Goriot, says to Paris, I said to London, '*à nous deux*.'[2] I desired to obtain a Professorship of either Physiology or Comparative Anatomy; and as vacancies occurred, I applied, but in vain. My friend, Professor Tyndall, and I were candidates at the same time, he for the Chair of Physics and I for that of Natural History, in the University of Toronto, which fortunately, as it turned out, would not look at either of us. I say fortunately, not from any lack of respect for Toronto, but because I soon made up my mind that London was the place for me, and hence I have steadily declined the inducements to leave it which have at various times been offered. At last, in 1854, on the translation of my warm friend, Edward Forbes, to Edinburgh, Sir Henry De la Beche, the Director-General of the Geological Survey, offered me the post Forbes vacated of Paleontologist and Lecturer on Natural History. I refused the former point blank, and accepted the latter provisionally, telling Sir Henry that I did not care for fossils, and that I should give up Natural History as soon as I could get a physiological post. But I held the office for thirty-one years, and a large part of my work has been paleontological.

At that time I disliked public speaking, and had a firm conviction that I should break down every time I opened my mouth. I believe I had every fault a speaker could have (except talking at random or indulging in rhetoric) when I spoke to the first important audience I ever addressed, on a Friday evening, at the Royal Institution, in 1852. Yet I must confess to having been guilty, *malgré moi*, of as much public speaking as most of my contemporaries, and for the last ten years it ceased to be so much of a bugbear to me. I used to pity myself for having to go through this training; but I am now more disposed to compassionate the unfortunate audiences, especially my ever friendly hearers at the Royal Institution, who were the subjects of my oratorical experiments.

The last thing that it would be proper for me to do would be to speak of the work of my life, or to say at the end of the day, whether I think I have earned my wages or not. Men are said to be partial judges of themselves—young men may be, I doubt if old men are. Life seems terribly foreshortened as they look back; and the mountain they set themselves to climb in youth turns out to be a mere spur of immeasurably higher ranges, when, with failing breath, they reach the top. But if I may speak of the objects I have had more or less definitely in view since I began the ascent of my hillock, they are briefly these: to promote the increase of natural knowledge and to forward the application of scientific methods of investigation to all the problems of life to the best of my ability, in the conviction—which has grown with my growth and strengthened with my strength—that there is no alleviation for the sufferings of mankind except veracity of thought and of action, and the resolute facing of the world as it is, when the garment of makebelieve, by which pious hands have hidden its uglier features, is stripped off.

It is with this intent that I have subordinated any reasonable or unreasonable ambition for scientific fame, which I may have permitted myself to entertain, to other ends; to the popularisation of science; to the development and organisation of scientific education; to the endless series of battles and skirmishes over evolution; and to untiring opposition to that ecclesiastical spirit, that clericalism, which in England, as everywhere else, and to whatever denomination it may belong, is the deadly enemy of science.

In striving for the attainment of these objects, I have been but one among many, and I shall be well content to be remembered, or even not remembered, as such. Circumstances, among which I am proud to reckon the devoted kindness of many friends, have led to my occupation of various prominent positions, among which the Presidency of the Royal Society[1] is the highest. It would be mock modesty on my part, with these and other scientific honours which have been bestowed upon me, to pretend that I have not succeeded in the career which I have followed, rather because I was driven into it, than of my own free will; but I am afraid I should not count even these things as marks of success, if I could not hope that I had somewhat helped that movement of opinion which has been called the New Reformation.

Speech at the Royal Society Dinner

BUT the most difficult task that remains is that which concerns myself. It is 43 years ago this day[1] since the Royal Society did me the honour to award me a Royal medal, and thereby determined my career. But, having long retired into the position of a veteran, I confess that I was extremely astonished—I honestly also say that I was extremely pleased to receive the announcement that you had been good enough to award to me the Darwin Medal.[2] But you know the Royal Society, like all things in this world, is subject to criticism. I confess that with the ingrained instincts of an old official that which arose in my mind after the reception of the information that I had been thus distinguished was to start an inquiry which I suppose suggests itself to every old official—How can my Government be justified? In reflecting upon what had been my own share in what are now very largely ancient transactions, it was perfectly obvious to me that I had no such claims as those of Mr. Wallace.[3] It was perfectly clear to me that I had no such claims as those of my life-long friend Sir Joseph Hooker,[4] who for 25 years placed all his great sources of knowledge, his sagacity, his industry, at the disposition of his friend Darwin. And really, I begin to despair of what possible answer could be given to the critics whom the Royal Society, meeting as it does on 30 November, has lately been very apt to hear about on 1 December. Naturally there occurred to my mind that famous and comfortable line, which I suppose has helped so many people under like circumstances, 'They also serve who only stand and wait.'[5] I am bound to confess that the standing and waiting, so far as I am concerned, to which I refer, has been of a somewhat peculiar character. I can only explain it, if you will permit me to narrate a story which came to me in my old nautical days, and which, I believe, has just as much foundation as a good deal of other information which I derived at the same period from the same source. There was a merchant ship in

110

which a member of the Society of Friends had taken passage, and that ship was attacked by a pirate, and the captain thereupon put into the hands of the member of the Society of Friends a pike, and desired him to take part in the subsequent action, to which, as you may imagine, the reply was that he would do nothing of the kind; but he said that he had no objection to stand and wait at the gangway. He did stand and wait with the pike in his hands, and when the pirates mounted and showed themselves coming on board he thrust his pike with the sharp end forward into the persons who were mounting, and he said, 'Friend, keep on board thine own ship.' It is in that sense that I venture to interpret the principle of standing and waiting to which I have referred. I was convinced as firmly as I have ever been convinced of anything in my life, that the *Origin of Species* was a ship laden with a cargo of rich value, and which, if she were permitted to pursue her course, would reach a veritable scientific Golconda, and I thought it my duty, however naturally averse I might be to fighting, to bid those who would disturb her beneficent operations to keep on board their own ship. If it has pleased the Royal Society to recognise such poor services as I may have rendered in that capacity, I am very glad, because I am as much convinced now as I was 34 years ago that the theory propounded by Mr. Darwin—I mean that which he propounded, not that which has been reported to be his by too many ill-instructed, both friends and foes—has never yet been shown to be inconsistent with any positive observations, and if I may use a phrase which I know has been objected to, and which I use in a totally different sense from that in which it was first proposed by its first propounder, I do believe that on all grounds of pure science it 'holds the field,' as the only hypothesis at present before us which has a sound scientific foundation. It is quite possible that you will apply to me the remark that has often been applied to persons in such a position as mine, that we are apt to exaggerate the importance of that to which our lives have been more or less devoted. But I am sincerely of opinion that the views which were propounded by Mr. Darwin 34 years ago may be understood hereafter as constituting an epoch in the intellectual history of the human race. They will modify the whole system of our thought and opinion, our most intimate convictions. But I do not know, I do not think anybody knows, whether the particular views which he held will be hereafter fortified by the experience of the ages which come after us; but of this thing I am perfectly certain, that the present course of things has resulted from the feeling of the smaller men who have followed him that they are incompetent to bend the bow of Ulysses, and in consequence many of them are seeking their salvation in mere speculation. Those who wish to attain to some clear and definite solution of the great problems which Mr. Darwin was the first person to set before us in later times must base themselves upon the facts which are stated in his great work, and, still more, must pursue their inquiries by the methods of which he was so brilliant an exemplar throughout the whole of his life. You must have his sagacity, his untiring search after the knowledge of fact, his readiness always to give up a preconceived opinion to that which was demonstrably true, before you can hope to carry his doctrines to their ultimate issue; and whether the particular form in which he has put them before us may be such as is finally destined to survive or not is more, I venture to think, than anybody is capable at this present moment of saying. But this one thing is perfectly certain—that it is only by pursuing his methods, by that wonderful single-mindedness, devotion to truth, readiness to sacrifice all things for the advance of definite knowledge, that we can hope to come any nearer than we are at present to the truths which he struggled to attain.

Explanatory Notes

===

DARWIN: AUTOBIOGRAPHICAL FRAGMENT

Page 3. (1) *Caroline:* Darwin's sister (see Index).
  (2) *Catherine:* Darwin's sister (see Index).
  (3) *damascenes:* 'Damask Prunes'; 'damascene' has given 'damson'.

Page 4. (1) *Parkfield:* the house of Mrs. Josiah Wedgwood I (see Index).
  (2) *my mother:* Susannah (see Index).
  (3) *Sarah and . . . Kitty:* Wedgwoods (see Index).
  (4) *Susan:* Darwin's sister (see Index).

Page 5. (1) *Mr. Case's School:* a day school in Shrewsbury kept by a Unitarian minister.
  (2) Cf. the *Autobiography, infra,* p. 9.

Page 6. (1) *Erasmus:* Darwin's brother (see Index).
  (2) *Dr. Butler's School:* Shrewsbury School; the headmaster was Samuel Butler (see Index). Darwin remained at the school until 1825.
  (3) *Plas Edwards:* at Towyn on the Welsh coast.

Page 7. *to Pistyll Rhaiadr. from Llyn Pen Rhiadr* down the Blyfnant to the Dovey.

DARWIN: AUTOBIOGRAPHY

Page 8. (1) *my Father:* Robert Waring Darwin (see Index).
  (2) *my mother:* Susannah (see Index).
  (3) *in Shrewsbury:* see *supra,* p. 5.

Page 10. *Dr. Butler:* see *supra,* p. 6, and Index.

Page 11. *Maer:* in Staffordshire, home of Josiah Wedgwood II (1769–1843), Darwin's uncle.

Page 16. *Sherburn:* see Index, Shelburn.

Page 22. (1) *my father's father:* Erasmus (see Index).
  (2) *Carlyle's Remembrances:* his *Reminiscences* (1881).

Page 23. my uncle: Samuel Tertius Galton (see Index).

Page 24. Henry and Parkes: authors respectively of *The Elements of Experimental Chemistry* (1823) and *Chemical Catechism* (1822).

Page 26. (1) *Wernerian:* Abraham Gottlob Werner (1750–1817), German mineralogist, founded the 'Neptunian' school which believed that all rocks of the earth's crust had been laid down under water.

(2) *Zoönomia: or The Laws of Organic Life* (1794–6).

Page 29. (1) *Mr. Owen:* possibly the Revd. Hugh Owen (1781–1827), author of *A History of Shrewsbury* (1825).

(2) *my Uncle Jos:* Josiah Wedgwood II (see Index).

Page 31. (1) *nec vultus tyranni* &c.: Horace, *Odes.* III. iii. 1–4: 'just and steady-purposed man, who mind is proof against clamouring mobs, despot's grimaces, the South wind of the Adriatic, or the crack and fall of Jupiter's heavens'.

(2) *Pearson on the Creed:* William Hodge Mill (1792–1853), *Analysis of the Exposition of the Creed by Pearson;* John Pearson (1613–86) was Bishop of Chester.

Page 32. Paley's . . . Philosophy: William Paley (1743–1805), author of *Moral and Political Philosophy* (1785), *Evidences of Christianity* (1794), and *Natural Theology* (1802); the essence of Anglican orthodoxy, prescribed reading in English universities until the mid-nineteenth century.

Page 33. (1) *I cannot remember:* Darwin's place was tenth.

(2) *Henslow:* see Index. For his influence on Darwin see *Darwin and Henslow. The Growth of an Idea. Letters 1831–1860*, ed. Nora Barlow (1967).

Page 40. Philosophical Magazine: xxi (1842), 180; 'Notes on the Effects produced by the Ancient Glaciers of Caernarvonshire, and on the Boulders transported by Floating Ice'.

Page 43. The first Lieutenant: John Clements Wickham, R.N., subsequently Governor of Queensland.

Page 44. (1) *Principles of Geology:* vol. i (1830), ii (1832), iii (1833). The second volume reached Darwin at Montevideo on 26 October 1832.

Page 47. letters . . . Cambridge: Extracts from Letters addressed to Professor Henslow by C. Darwin Esq. privately reprinted by Sydney Smith (1960).

Page 54. This conclusion . . . weaker: added from an autograph note in Francis Darwin's copy.

Page 56. your Mother: Emma (Wedgwood) Darwin (see Index).

Page 57. in London: the Darwins' first home was 12 Upper Gower Street, subsequently renumbered 110 Gower Street; destroyed by a German bomb in 1941. The site is now occupied by an extension of University College, London.

Page 58. (1) *papers:* 'On the Distribution of the Erratic Boulders and on the Contemporaneous Unstratified Deposits of South America', *Proceedings of the Geological Society,* iii (1842), 425; 'On the Connexion of certain Volcanic Phenomena and on the Formation of Mountain-Chains and the Effects of Continental Elevations', *Transactions of the Geol. Soc.,* v (1840), 601; 'On the Formation of Mould', *Proc. Geol. Soc.,* ii (1838), 574.

(2) *Zoology of the Voyage of the Beagle:* published in five parts by R. Owen, G. R. Waterhouse, J. Gould, L. Jenyns, and T. Bell, under Darwin's editorship, between 1839 and 1843.

(3) *Philosophical Magazine:* see *supra,* note to p. 40.

Page 61. You will find him out: examples of Richard Owen's malice and dishonesty are given in Sir Gavin de Beer, *Charles Darwin* (1963).

Page 63. (1) *Ehrenberg:* see Index. His blunders appear to relate to his attribution to unicellular organisms of organs which they have been found not to possess.

(2) *Agassiz:* see Index. He believed that 'the forms of life which have successfully tenanted the globe were the incarnations of successive thoughts of the Deity and that He wiped out one set of these embodiments by an appalling geological catastrophe as soon as His ideas took a more advanced shape'. *Life and Letters of T.H.H.,* i (1900), 169; small wonder that Huxley smote at him.

Page 65. (1) *History of Civilisation: in England* (1857–61).

(2) *Effie:* Katherine Euphemia Wedgwood (see Index).

Page 66. Carlyle: see Index. 'Jeremiah with castanets' (Logan Pearsall Smith's opinion with which Darwin would have agreed).

Page 67. Goethe: His *Theory of Colours* is worthless.

Page 69. Cirripedia: barnacles.

Page 71. (1) My first note-book: see Chronology, p. xxiii.

(2) *In June 1842* &c.: Darwin's Sketch of 1842 and his Essay of 1844 were published as *The Foundations of the Origin of Species* (1909); reprinted in Sir Gavin de Beer, *Evolution by Natural Selection* (1958).

Page 73. the Origin of Species: not only the demonstration of evolution by natural selection, but the starting-point of the science of ecology of which Darwin was a founding father by his proof that efficient adaptation to the conditions of the environment was the criterion for survival by natural selection of favourable variations.

Page 74. (1) *the close resemblance . . . class:* the resemblance of embryos and the differences between embryos and adults is dealt with by Sir Gavin de Beer, 'Darwin's views on the relations between embryology and evolution', *Journal of the Linnean Society of London*, xliv (1958), 15–23.

(2) *Häckel:* his enthusiasm for evolution led him to make the most unwarrantable assumptions about the significance of ancestors for the development of embryos (see Sir Gavin de Beer, *Embryos and Ancestors,* 1962).

Page 79. (1) *the Expression of the Emotions* &c.: made Darwin a pioneer in the study of animal behaviour and the science of ethology.

(2) *My first child:* William Erasmus Darwin was the subject of Darwin's study, 'A biographical Sketch of an Infant', *Mind,* vii (July 1877).

(3) *Hartfield:* in Sussex, where 'The Ridge' was the home of Sarah Elizabeth Wedgwood (1793–1880), sister of Darwin's wife.

Page 80. The Effects of . . . Self-Fertilisation: contains the results of the first experimental demonstration of the superior vigour of hybrids over inbred offspring; it provides the explanation of the survival value in evolution of the existence of two separate sexes.

Page 81. (1) *Frank:* Francis, Darwin's son (see Index).

(2) *Power of Movement in Plants:* contains the results of Darwin's experiments on the effects of light on the tip of a plant shoot which demonstrated the existence of 'some matter in the upper part which is acted upon by light, and which transmits its effects to the lower part'. From this experiment stemmed the whole science of growth-promoting substances and hormones in plants.

(3) *The Formation of Vegetable Mould . . . Worms:* of the greatest

importance for agriculture (see Sir Albert Howard, intro. to *Darwin on Humus and the Earthworm*, 1965), completely neglected by the excessive use of artificial chemical manures which kill the worms.

Page 87. heterostylism: the condition in which a species of plant has some flowers with short styles and others with long styles; the phenomenon is mentioned in connexion with *Linum, Primula,* and *Lythrum* on pp. 76–7, and is treated in Darwin's *Different Forms of Flowers on Plants of the same Species* (1877).

Heterostylism (now *heterostyly*) is an adaptation, as Darwin discovered, tending to ensure outcrossing, since long styles are correlated with a low position of the anthers in the flower, and short styles with a high position of the anthers. Since the flowers are fertilized by the insertion of the proboscis of an insect, such a flower is normally pollinated from a different flower, often from a different plant, resulting in outcrossing.

Page 88. Hopedene: in Surrey, the home of Hensleigh Wedgwood, Darwin's brother-in-law.

HUXLEY: NOTEBOOK, 'THOUGHTS AND DOINGS'

Page 91. (1) MS. Imperial College of Science and Technology, Huxley Papers 31. 69.

(2) *Hinckley:* twelve miles from Coventry.

(3) *Dr. S. Smith:* Sydney Smith (1771–1845), Canon of St. Paul's.

Page 92. (1) *May:* George Anderson May lived at Hinckley.

(2) *Cogito, ergo sum:* Descartes' proof of his own existence; *Discours de la Méthode* (1637).

Page 93. (1) *Muller's Physiology: Elements of Physiology,* English transl. (1840).

(2) *Hume: History of Great Britain* (1754–61).

Page 94. (1) *Macintosh:* Sir James Mackintosh (1765–1832), *History of England* (1830).

(2) *Guizot: History of Civilisation in Europe,* English transl. (1837).

(3) *Turner:* Edward Turner, *Elements of Chemistry* (1827).

Page 95. Robertson: William Robertson, *History of Scotland* (1759).

Page 96. Huxley has written 'first' and added '2'.

Page 97. (1) *Paracelsus:* 1835; *Sordello:* 1840.

(2) *Festus:* 1839. It will be noted from this reading-list that Huxley was up to date with poetical publication. Horne's epic poem *Orion* appeared in 1843.

Page 98. a journal: text from Leonard Huxley, *Life and Letters of Thomas Henry Huxley* (1900), i. 15–16.

HUXLEY AUTOBIOGRAPHY

Page 101. (1) *my mother:* Rachel Withers (*ob.* 1852).

(2) *my father:* George Huxley.

Page 102. Sir Herbert Oakley: see Index. As Oakeley was one of the first clergy to introduce religious education by the system of Sunday schools, and as he had frequent difficulties with nonconformists over the payment of church rates, his effect on Huxley's opinions may be recognized in the latter's disapproval of dissenters (p. 92) being charged these rates, and in his advocacy of the retention of Bible teaching in elementary education (p. xvii).

Page 103. (1) *a medical brother-in-law:* Dr. Cooke, husband of Huxley's sister Ellen.

(2) *kind people:* the family of Jaggard, living at Grove Fields.

Page 104. my first scientific paper: 'On a hitherto undescribed Structure in the Human Hair-sheath', *London Medical Gazette*, i (1845), 1340.

Page 106. Stanley: see Index. Huxley wrote of him: 'The young Commander has raised an enduring monument in his works, and his epitaph shall be the grateful thanks of many a mariner threading his way among the mazes of the Coral Sea'; he died in Huxley's arms, aboard his ship, in Sydney harbour.

Page 107. (1) *a more elaborate paper:* on Stanley's suggestion, sent to his father Edward Stanley, Bishop of Norwich (F.R.S. 1840), for forwarding to the Royal Society. It was entitled 'On the Anatomy and Affinities of the family of the Medusae'; *Philosophical Transactions*, ii (1849), 413.

(2) *à nous deux:* a reference to the climax of Balzac's novel *Le Père Goriot* (1834) where the disillusioned Rastignac, after the burial of old Goriot at Père Lachaise Cemetery, looks down on Paris from the summit of Père Lachaise and issues his challenge: 'Now the contest is between us two.'

Page 109. *Presidency of the Royal Society:* 5 July 1883 to 30 November 1885.

HUXLEY: SPEECH AT THE ROYAL SOCIETY DINNER

Page 110. (1) *43 years ago this day:* Huxley was mistaken by one year; it was in 1852 that he was awarded a Royal Medal, but he narrowly missed one in 1851.

(2) *the Darwin Medal:* awarded on that same day, 30 November 1894.

(3) *Mr. Wallace:* (see Index) awarded the first Darwin Medal in 1890.

(4) *Hooker:* (see Index) awarded the Darwin Medal in 1892.

(5) *They also serve . . . wait:* Milton, Sonnet xvi; on his blindness.

Index

Agassiz, Jean-Louis-Rodolphe, 1807–73, For. Mem. R.S. 1837, 49, 63

Ainsworth, William Francis, 1807–96, geologist and surgeon, 26

Armstrong, Sir Alexander, 1818–99, F.R.S. 1873, 106

Audubon, John James, 1785–1851, F.R.S. 1830, ornithologist, 28

Babbage, Charles, 1792–1871, F.R.S. 1816, mathematician and astronomer; inventor of a calculating machine, 63–4, 66

Beaumont, Léonce Elie de, 1798–1874, For. Mem. R.S. 1835, 59

Bell, Lady Caroline, wife of Sir John Bell, 1782–1876, Chief Secretary of the Government of the Cape of Good Hope, 63

Bell, Sir Charles, 1774–1842, F.R.S. 1826, author of *The Anatomy and Philosophy of Expression as connected with the Fine Arts*, 79

Beneden, Pierre-Joseph van, 1809–94, For. Mem. R.S. 1875, embryologist, 87

Brown, Robert, 1773–1858, F.R.S. 1811, naturalist; discoverer of the cell nucleus and of 'Brownian movement', 48, 60–1, 76

Buckland, Rev. William, 1784–1856, F.R.S. 1818, geologist, 60

Buckle, Henry Thomas, 1821–62, historian, 64, 65

Bulwer, Sir Edward Lytton, later Lord Lytton, 1803–73, essayist and novelist, 69

Burnett, Sir William, 1779–1861, F.R.S. 1833, 105

Butler, Dr. Samuel, 1774–1839; F.R.S. 1822; Bishop of Lichfield 1836, 6, 10, 24

Butler, Samuel, 1835–1902, author of *Erehwon* and of demented attacks on CD's integrity and work, 81

Carlyle, Thomas, 1795–1881, 66–7, 96

Case, Rev. G., Unitarian minister, 5–6

Castlereagh, Lord, 41, 44

Clark, Sir Andrew, Bart., 1826–93, F.R.S. 1885, 106

Coldstream, Dr. John, 1806–63, physician, 26, 27

Cork and Orrery, Countess of, *née* Mary Monckton, 1746–1840, 'blue stocking', 65

Darwin, Annie, *d.* 1851, CD's daughter, 57

Darwin, Caroline Sarah, 1800–88, CD's sister, married 1837 Josiah Wedgwood II, Mrs. Darwin's brother, 3, 8–9, 29

Darwin, Charles, 1809–82 (in T. H. Huxley's 'Speech'), 110, 111, 112

Darwin, Emily Catherine, 1810–66, CD's sister, married 1863 Charles Langton, 3, 4, 9

Darwin, Erasmus, 1731–1802, F.R.S. 1761, CD's grandfather, physician philosopher, poet inventor; author of *Zoönomia, The Temple of Nature*, etc., 22, 26, 81

Darwin, Erasmus Alvey, 1804–81, CD's brother, 6, 7, 22, 25, 26, 50

Darwin, Francis, 1848–1925, F.R.S. 1882, CD's son, 81

Darwin, Dr. Robert Waring, 1766–1848, CD's father, F.R.S. 1788, 8, 12–22, 24–6, 31, 40–1, 45, 50, 55, 69, 82

Darwin, Susan Elizabeth, 1803–66, CD's sister, 4

Darwin, Susannah, 1765–1817, CD's mother; daughter of Josiah Wedgwood I, 4, 8

Dawes, Rev. Richard, 1793–1867, F.R.S. 1815, fourth Wrangler, educationist, 38

De la Beche, Sir Henry Thomas, 1796–1855, F.R.S. 1819, 108

Duncan, Andrew, 1773–1832, 25

Ehrenberg, Christian Gottfried, 1795–1876, For. Mem. R.S. 1837, zoologist, 63

Eyton, Thomas Campbell, 1809–80, naturalist, 38

Falconer, Hugh, 1808–65, F.R.S. 1845, palaeontologist, 61

Fayrer, Sir Joseph, Bart., 1824–1907, F.R.S. 1833, 105

Fitzroy, Capt. Robert, R.N., 1805–65, later Admiral, 40, 41–4, 45, 47, 68

Forbes, Edward, 1815–54, F.R.S. 1845, naturalist, 74, 108

Fox, Rev. William Darwin, c. 1805–80, CD's second cousin, 35

Galton, Francis, 1822–1911, CD's first cousin, F.R.S. 1856, knighted 1909, founder of eugenics, 22

Galton, Samuel Tertius, CD's uncle, 22

George, H.R.H. Prince, Duke of Cambridge, 1819–1904, 102

Grant, Dr. Robert Edmund, 1793–1874, F.R.S. 1836, zoologist, 26, 27

Gray, Rev. Asa, 1810–88, botanist; CD's staunch supporter on evolution in the U.S., 72, 74, 77

Grote, George, 1794–1871, F.R.S. 1857; author of *History of Greece*, 1846–56, 66

Häckel, Ernst, 1834–1919, zoologist, 74

Haughton, Rev. Samuel, 1821–97, F.R.S. 1858, Professor of Geology, Dublin University, 72

Henslow, Rev. John Stevens, 1796–1861, botanist, 33, 36–7, 38, 39, 40, 41, 47, 48, 59

Herbert, John Maurice, 1808–82, County Court Judge in South Wales, 34

Herschel, Sir John, 1792–1871, F.R.S. 1813: *Introduction to the [A Preliminary Discourse on the] Study of Natural Philosophy*, 38, 63

Hill, Major William Noel, 3rd Lord Berwick, d. 1842, 29

Hooker, Joseph Dalton, 1817–1911, F.R.S. 1847, later Knight and Director of Royal Botanic Gardens, Kew, 47, 61, 62, 68, 72, 74, 110

Hope, Thomas Charles, 1766–1844, F.R.S. 1810, 25

Horner, Leonard, 1785–1864, F.R.S. 1813, geologist, 28

Humboldt, Alexander von, 1769–1859, For. Mem. R.S. 1815, traveller and naturalist, 38, 63, 91

Huth, Alfred Henry, 1850–1910, author of *Marriages of Near Kin*, 1875, 87

Huxley, George, THH's father, 92, 101

Huxley, Rachel Withers, d. 1852, THH's mother, 92, 101

Huxley, Thomas Henry, 1825–95 (in Darwin's *Autobiography*), 62, 68, 75, 81, 84

Jameson, Professor Robert, 1774–1854, founder of the Wernerian Society 1808, 27, 28, 29

Jenyns, Rev. Leonard (afterwards Blomefield), 1800–93, zoologist, 37

Jones, Thomas Wharton, 1808–91, F.R.S. 1840, 104

Kay-Shuttleworth, James Philip, 1804–77, physician, statesman, 27
Kingsley, Rev. Charles, 1819–75, Canon of Westminster, 67

Lamarck, Jean-Baptiste de, 1744–1829, author of *Philosophie zoologique*, 1809; soldier, botanist, and zoologist; first to draw up a coherent theory of evolution (but with erroneous explanation), 26, 59
Lavater, Johann Caspar, 1741–1831, author of *Essays on Physiognomy*, (Eng. transl. 1804), 41
Leighton, Rev. William Allport, 1805–89, 9
Litchfield, Richard Buckley, 1832–1903 (married 1871 CD's daughter Henrietta Emma), 81
Lyell, Lady Charles, *née* Mary Horner, Leonard's daughter, 1808–73, 59
Lyell, Sir Charles, 1797–1875, F.R.S. 1826, 17, 44, 47, 48, 58–9, 60, 66, 70, 72, 74, 75

Macaulay, Thomas Babington, 1800–59, F.R.S. 1849, historian and statesman, 65, 66
Macgillivray, William, 1796–1852, naturalist, 29
Mackintosh, Sir James, 1765–1832, F.R.S. 1813, philosopher, lawyer, and author; brother-in-law of Josiah Wedgwood II, 30, 37, 94
Malthus, Thomas Robert, 1766–1834, F.R.S. 1818, 71
Miller, Professor William Hallowes, 1801–80, F.R.S. 1838, fifth Wrangler, mineralogist, 48
Milman, Rev. Henry Hart, 1791–1868, Dean of St. Paul's, 65
Milnes, Richard Monckton, later Lord

Houghton, 1809–85, F.R.S. 1868, *littérateur* and politician, 66, 97
Mivart, St. George Jackson, 1827–1900, F.R.S. 1869, biologist; treated CD's works in flagrant bad faith, 75
Monro, Alexander, 1773–1859, 25
Motley, John Lothrop, 1814–77, author of *History of the Dutch Republics*, 1856, 66
Müller, Fritz [Friedrich], 1822–97, naturalist, 74
Murchison, Sir Roderick Impey, 1792–1871, F.R.S. 1826, geologist, 60, 63

Oakley [Oakeley], Rev. Sir Herbert, 3rd Bart. (1791–1845), Vicar of Ealing 1822–34, later Archdeacon of Colchester, 102
Owen, Richard, 1804–92, F.R.S. 1834, anatomist, later Superintendant of the Natural History Dept. of the British Museum, 61, 63

Paley, William, 1743–1805, 32, 33, 50
Petty, William, Earl of Shelburn, 1st Marquis of Lansdowne, 1737–1805, 16–17
Petty-Fitzmaurice, Henry, 3rd Marquis of Lansdowne, 1780–1863, F.R.S. 1811, 17

Ramsay, Marmaduke, c. 1799–1831, fifteenth Wrangler, 37, 38
Richardson, Sir John, 1787–1865, F.R.S. 1825, surgeon to Sir John Franklin's two Polar expeditions, 105–6

Scott, Sir Walter, 28
Sedgwick, Rev. Adam, 1785–1873, F.R.S. 1821, geologist, 33, 39–40, 47, 59
Shelburn, Earl of: see Petty
Smith, Rev. Sydney, 1771–1845, Canon of St. Paul's, 65, 66, 91

Index

Spencer, Herbert, 1820–1903, philosopher, 53, 64, 65, 102

Sprengel, Christian Konrad, 1750–1816, plant breeder and experimenter on the fertilization of flowers, 75

Stanhope, Philip Henry, 4th Earl Stanhope, 1781–1855, 66

Stanhope, Philip Henry, 5th Earl Stanhope, 1805–75, historian, 65, 66

Stanley, Captain Owen, R.N., 1811–50, F.R.S. 1842, 106

Stephen, Rev. Leslie, 1832–1904, philosopher, alpinist, editor of Dictionary of National Biography, and father of Virginia Woolf and Vanessa Bell, 81

Stephens, James Francis, 1792–1852, 35

Stuart, Charles Edward Sobieski, 1799–1880; real name Allan, subsequently Stuart Allan, subsequently Allan Stuart, 41

Thompson, Harry Stephen Meysey, 1809–74, agriculturalist, later Baronet, 35

Turner, Dawson William?, 1815–85, 38

Tyler [Tylor], Edward, 1832–1917, F.R.S. 1871, anthropologist; author of Primitive Culture, 1871, 53

Tyndall, John, 1820–93, F.R.S. 1852, physicist, glaciologist, and alpinist, 108

Wallace, Alfred Russel, 1823–1913, F.R.S. 1893, naturalist, socialist, and spiritualist, 72, 74, 110

Wallich, George Charles, 1815–99, naturalist and oceanographer, 41

Waterton, Charles, 1782–1865, naturalist, 28

Watt-Reid, Sir John, 1823–1909, 106

Way, Albert, 1805–74, Director of the Society of Antiquaries 1842–6, 35

Wedgwood, Catherine, 1774–1823, CD's aunt, 'Aunt Kitty', 4, 56

Wedgwood, Emma, later Mrs. Charles Darwin, 56, 68

Wedgwood, Hensleigh, 1803–91, brother of CD's wife, 64

Wedgwood, Josiah (II), 1769–1843, CD's uncle and father-in-law, 29, 30, 40, 44

Wedgwood, Mrs. Josiah (I), d. 1815, CD's grandmother, 4

Wedgwood, Katherine Euphemia, b. 1839, Emma Darwin's niece, married 1873 Sir Thomas (later Lord) Farrer, 65

Wedgwood, Sarah Elizabeth, 1778–1856, CD's aunt, 4

Whewell, Rev. William, 1794–1866; F.R.S. 1820; Master of Trinity College; author of History of the Inductive Sciences 1837, 37, 61

White, Gilbert, author of The Natural History of Selborne, 1789, 24

Whitley, Rev. Charles Thomas 1808–95, reader in natural philosophy and Hon. Canon of Durham, 33–4

Wickham, John Clements, R.N., later Governor of Queensland, n. to p. 43